£2 childrens

KT-133-040

CRY OF THE TIGER

This book is dedicated to Michael Wright,
who continues to call out in the
wilderness . . .

CRY OF THE TIGER

The Amazing True Story of
Tony Anthony
a Kung Fu World Champion

Angela Little

Authentic

MILTON KEYNES ● COLORADO SPRINGS ● HYDERABAD

Copyright © 2006 Angela Little and Tony Anthony

14 13 12 11 10 09 08   8 7 6 5 4 3 2
This edition first printed 2008, reprinted 2008

First published 2006 by Authentic Media,
9 Holdom Avenue, Bletchley, Milton Keynes, Bucks., MK1 1QR, UK
1820 Jet Stream Drive, Colorado Springs, CO 80921, USA
OM Authentic Media, Medchal Road, Jeedimetla Village, Secunderabad 500 055,
A.P., India
www.authenticmedia.co.uk
Authentic Media is a division of IBS-STL UK., a company limited by guarantee,
with its Registered Office at Kingstown Broadway, Carlisle, Cumbria CA3 0HA.
Registered in England & Wales
No. 1216232. Registered charity 270162

The right of Angela Little to be identified as the Author of this Work has
been asserted by her in accordance with the Copyright, Designs and
Patents Act 1988.

All rights reserved. No part of this publication may be reproduced,
stored in a retrieval system, or transmitted in any form or
by any means, electronic, mechanical, photocopying, recording or
otherwise, without the prior permission of the publisher or a licence
permitting restricted copying. In the UK such licences are issued by the
Copyright Licensing Agency,
90 Tottenham Court Road, London, W1P 9HE.

British Library Cataloguing in Publication Data

A catalogue record for this book is available from the
British Library

ISBN 978-1-86024-708-8

Cover design by Mark Baker
Print Management by Adare Carwin
Printed in Great Britain by J.H. Haynes & Co., Sparkford

ACKNOWLEDGEMENTS

Angela Little and Tony Anthony first collaborated on the award-winning book *Taming the Tiger*. Today Tony travels the world telling his story; *Cry of the Tiger* is another chapter in his ongoing journey.

There are many people to thank: Malcolm Down and the team at Authentic Media; Su Box for her patience and skill as an editor; and Joshua Griggs, Nicole Griggs, Joseph Palmer, Bethany Taylor and Laura Cross for their helpful feedback on the manuscript.

With love and special thanks also to friends and precious family, without whose support this would not have been possible . . . and finally to you, the reader, for taking the time to join us on the journey.

CONTENTS

1

FAR FROM HOME

Tony woke with a start. The plane was banking steeply, beginning its descent into Hong Kong Airport. He peered through the little window beside him and looked down at the clouds. The drone of the engines vibrated harshly through his head as he pressed his nose harder against the glass. Were they above land or sea? He couldn't tell. Was it always this blue up here? Does the sun always shine above the clouds? Tony wondered. He squinted against the yellow light, trying to find a gap in the cotton wool carpet billowing beneath.

For a few moments Tony lost himself in the magic of the sky, but soon his ears were popping, filling his head with a dull ache. Their long journey was coming to an end. Suddenly there was no more blue, no more sunshine. They were flying through the thick of the cloud. Now all Tony could see was a reflection in the glass – the shadowy image of the thin stranger sitting next to him.

A chill ran through him. Just who was this man? Where was he taking him? Tony's eyes pricked with tears and he swallowed hard, remembering their first meeting . . .

'I want you to be a good boy,' his mother had told him sternly. 'This man is going to take you to live with your grandfather in China.'

Her words hung in the air like a mighty storm cloud.

His mother crouched down and looked into his eyes, taking both his hands in hers.

'Your father is ill and we can't afford to look after you any more,' she said. For a moment Tony thought she might pull him close, hugging him the way he longed for her to do, but she didn't.

'It will be better this way,' she said, now standing and turning back to talk to the stranger. She spoke in Chinese. Tony didn't understand. Suddenly his heart was pounding in his chest. What was wrong with Dad? What was all this about? Why did he have to go away? Questions bombarded his head, but he didn't know where to start. He turned to look at his father who was slouching forward in his chair, staring into the empty black fireplace.

'Dad, wha–' Tony stuttered, but before he could say anything more the stranger gripped his wrist. Instinctively Tony pulled away, but his mother gave him one of her harsh looks. His heart thundered. He wanted to shout, to cry, but he didn't. The stranger led him outside. The nightmare was only just beginning.

✛   ✛   ✛

Hong Kong Airport was like nowhere Tony had ever been before. There were peculiar smells and the air was thick and humid. The stranger gripped his arm tightly, leading him hurriedly through a crowd of people clamouring to collect their baggage. Tony felt small and invisible as bags, boxes and trolleys knocked into him. He struggled to keep up and his eyes darted around, like those of a frightened rabbit, looking for something, or someone, familiar.

Bang! A painful shove knocked Tony to the floor. A large suitcase hit him in the chest, leaving him gasping for air. The stranger shouted in Chinese and yanked Tony to his feet.

'Wait, please wait, just a minute,' Tony panted, his head dizzy, but the stranger wasn't listening. He grasped Tony tighter around his wrist, making his fingers turn purple as they hurried on through the crowd.

All of a sudden they stopped. Tony was relieved to catch his breath, but now they were stuck. The crowd thickened. People started pushing and shouting. Tony's face nudged hard against the stranger's legs. He stood on tiptoe, but still couldn't see what the hold-up was. Then there was a terrifying screeching noise, and flapping right behind him. Spinning round in fear, Tony saw a cage full of birds, their wings whipping as they slammed themselves against the bars, eyes wide, beaks stabbing in frenzy. He let out a cry and the old witch-like woman carrying the cage laughed at him, revealing a wide, toothless grin.

Tony shrank back from the flaying feathers, again feeling a sharp yank from his guardian. The crowd was thinning now. Soon Tony saw what the hold-up had been. There was a party of school children. Seeing the young foreigner, some of them started pointing and laughing.

Why are they pointing at me? Tony wondered. He stared back indignantly. All the children looked the same. They had straight black hair and wore green tunics with matching caps, red neckerchiefs and flip-flops on their feet. It was then Tony realized how different he must appear to them. He had some of his mother's oriental features, but his hair was thick and wavy and his eyes more rounded, like his father's. He wore blue jeans, trainers, a sweater and a heavy anorak that must have looked very strange to the Chinese children.

Finally they broke free of the crowd, out into the open, but Tony barely had chance to take in his surroundings. Before he knew what was going on he was hoisted aboard a horse-drawn cart. Tony was lifted up to sit beside an old man dressed in black who held onto the reins. The man didn't say a word. He didn't even look at Tony or smile. Tony remembered what his mother had told him. 'You are going to live with your grandfather.' Could this be him? He stole a glance at the man. He was wiry, with dark, leathery skin and a thin grey moustache. Surely his grandfather would be pleased to see him? Tony chewed nervously at his lip. The guardian jumped onto the back of the cart and they pulled away. Tony shuddered in fear. Why wasn't anyone speaking to him? Where were they going? Would he ever see his home and his family again?

Tony felt queasy at the rocking motion of the cart and he swallowed hard to make the sickness stay in the pit of his stomach. On and on they rode, through a mysterious landscape of paddy fields and roadside shacks that soon turned into eerie black shadows of night.

✛   ✛   ✛

At last the horse halted. The guardian lifted Tony down and pushed him ahead into a strange house. Tony blinked as his eyes grew accustomed to the pale light. What was this place? An old woman greeted him. She was small, with grey hair tied neatly in a bun at the back of her head.

'Jowmo,' the woman said, pointing to herself and smiling. Tony felt a small flicker of warmth inside him. He had been so frightened on the journey. Perhaps now things would get better. This must be his grandmother. He smiled back shyly, but to his alarm the woman's face suddenly grew stern as the wiry man with the moustache came in.

'Lowsi,' the woman said, gesturing towards him. With that, she put both hands together and made a small bow. Instinctively Tony did the same and Lowsi gave him a short nod of approval.

The man soon disappeared and Tony was relieved to be left alone with Jowmo. She chatted in a high-pitched twang, but he couldn't understand anything she said. Although Tony's mother was Chinese, they only ever spoke English at home. Seating him at a small wooden table, Jowmo put a bowl of steaming liquid in front of him. It was like nothing he had seen or smelled before – a thin broth of floating vegetables and noodles. Tony realized he was hungry and patiently waited for a spoon. A few moments later Jowmo turned and looked at him as if wondering why he was not eating. Then she laughed. Taking another bowl, she cupped it in her hands, lifted it to her lips and drank from it, slurping the noodles between her teeth. Tony smiled and copied.

He didn't much care for the taste, but there was something comforting about the warmth of the soup. Between slurps he looked around, taking in the unfamiliar surroundings. There was very little furniture and the space seemed to be separated into different rooms by only bamboo screens. Big pictures of black and white Chinese script decorated the walls and there were lots of small tables with strange-looking fruit or fresh flowers in neat vases.

Tony drained the last of the broth from the bowl and struggled to stifle a yawn. Jowmo spotted it and laid her head on her hands, gesturing that it was time to sleep. Tony nodded gratefully. She took him through to another area of the house and pulled back one of the bamboo screens, revealing a small room with a single wooden chair and a small bench in one corner. Was this his bed? It reminded him of the garden seat they had at home! Jowmo handed him a grey tunic then, with a brief smile, she said something Tony didn't understand and left.

He was alone. Looking around the bare room he fingered the tunic and thought about his superhero pyjamas and his bed, covered with soft toys, back home. A few tears escaped down his cheek and he pushed his thoughts to the back of his mind. Exhausted, he lay down for a deep, but haunted sleep.

2

LIVING NIGHTMARE

Splash!

Tony leaped from his sleep as a bucket of ice-cold water came crashing over his head. Where was he? A man was shouting.

'*Lo han quilo! Lo han quilo!*' (Little foreign devil!)

Then he remembered. It was still dark, but Tony could make out the figure of Lowsi, his grandfather. The empty bucket crashed to the floor. Tony cowered in the corner as the old man thwacked his bamboo cane, making harsh slapping noises on the edge of the bed. He felt a rush of air on his face as the cane lashed dangerously close.

What should he do? What did Lowsi want with him? Tony couldn't understand what he was shouting. Desperation gripped him and, in fear of the cane, he leaped off the hard bamboo bed and scrambled to his feet. Immediately Lowsi's shouting stopped. Grabbing Tony by his arm he dragged him roughly through the house and out into the open.

Everything was shrouded in shadowy darkness, but he could see they were in some kind of courtyard. What had Tony done wrong? Why was his grandfather so angry with him? The bitter early morning wind whipped through his thin sleeping tunic like a razor. Lowsi's strong fingers gripped his shoulders, rooting him to the spot. Tony shivered as the icy drops of water ran down his face and body making tiny puddles on the floor, but he didn't move.

Silence fell over the courtyard.

What was happening? A mixture of fear and curiosity helped him forget the cold, but Tony still trembled as he fixed his eyes on his grandfather.

What was he doing? The old man walked a little way off and then turned to face him. He stood very still, eerily still, for what seemed like a very long time. Tony squinted through the half-light at his grandfather's face. His eyes were closed. Was he sleeping? Then Lowsi began to move. Very slowly, like a cat unfurling herself, he began stretching out his arms and legs, making strange shapes with his hands. His eyes stayed shut, but Tony had a strange sense that the old man was still watching him.

Lowsi's weird activity went on and on. After some time, Tony let his eyes wander around the courtyard. It was a peculiar place. There was a mysterious-looking gate at the far end and, beyond, a dense, forbidding forest. Tony's mind flashed back to his home back in London. Everything here was so different.

He glanced up. Strange-shaped decorations looked as if they were dancing on the edge of the roof. There were dragons, horses with wings and unicorns (like he had seen in his picture books), a huge bird surrounded by fire and something that looked like a man riding a hen!

Thwack! Tony heard the sound just a moment before he felt the sting. He had barely taken his eyes off Lowsi. Now his face was smarting where it had been struck by the old man's cane. *Whap!* There it was again, harder this time. Tony's head spun. He swallowed hard, seeing tiny splashes of red blood splattering his tunic.

'Don't cry. I won't cry. I won't cry,' Tony said to himself. Somehow he knew that would only make it worse. His eyes pricked with tears, but he dug his fingernails into his palms and braced himself. Lowsi stood over him, the bamboo cane in his wiry hands. What had he done to deserve such a harsh beating? Something told him not to ask.

After that every morning was the same. Tony quickly learned to avoid the icy bath by waking long before dawn. When Lowsi came into his room he was always up and ready. He greeted him with a respectfully low bow. Lowsi was his grandfather, but more than that he was his master – someone to be obeyed at all times. Out in the courtyard Tony kept his attention locked on his strange moves. Sometimes his eyelids felt so heavy, he longed to close them and drift off to sleep. But if he even blinked too heavily Lowsi's cane was thwacked across his ears.

As the weeks went by Tony began to pick up his grandparents' Cantonese dialect and Lowsi began teaching him about the way of his ancestors.

'Kung fu has been in our family for over five hundred years,' Lowsi told him. 'It is an ancient way that has been passed down through the generations.' Tony listened intently, knowing that he must learn quickly if he were to avoid a beating.

'Kung fu is a martial art that was introduced to China by an Indian monk. We Chinese know him as Ta Mo. He came here at the beginning of the sixth century to spread the teachings of Buddha throughout China.'

Tony wasn't sure what a martial art was, but clearly it was something important. He had heard Jowmo and Lowsi speak of Buddha a great deal. Maybe he was some sort of god. He wasn't sure about that either. There were so many things to learn about this strange new country.

'While wandering in the mountains of northern China, Ta Mo stopped at a monastery called Shaolin,' Lowsi continued. 'There he encouraged the monks to meditate and seek enlightenment. But the monks often fell asleep as they meditated – so the wise teacher gave them exercises to help keep them awake. These became a meditation in themselves, but they were also very powerful fighting moves.'

Fighting? Like his father used to watch on TV? Tony wondered. He looked questioningly at his grandfather.

'The moves that Ta Mo taught helped defend the monks from bandits as they travelled between monasteries,' Lowsi explained.

As he spoke, Lowsi began shaping Tony's body into the positions he made in the courtyard each morning. Soon Tony was joining in the strange slow movements, twisting his hands, arms and legs in imitation of his grandfather. He found it difficult at first and kept losing his balance. Sometimes it felt as though his bones were bending as Lowsi forced his body into different positions.

'This is t'ai chi,' Lowsi told him, shaping Tony's arms into another painful pose. 'It is the basis of the kung fu exercises that Ta Mo taught our Shaolin ancestors.'

The next day was the same, and the one after that, and Tony gradually learned how to make some of the moves without Lowsi's help. T'ai chi was now part of his daily routine. The moves were difficult, but there was another part of the teaching that Tony found even harder. Hour after hour he was made to stand perfectly still, holding a position until his muscles ached and his limbs quivered uncontrollably, desperate to move.

'The way of kung fu is much more than physical strength and fighting moves,' Lowsi had explained. 'At the heart of martial arts is the chi. This is the life force we believe is within everyone and everything. To master kung fu is to harness the chi; through it, you will become extremely powerful.'

Tony hadn't really understood what his grandfather was talking about, but he hadn't dared say so.

'Now concentrate on your breathing,' Lowsi had instructed sternly. 'This time focus on the chi that is within you.' With that he'd walked away, again leaving Tony to stand motionless for what seemed like an eternity.

✠   ✠   ✠

One morning after the t'ai chi exercises, Lowsi placed a bucket of sand in front of Tony. What was that for?

Suddenly Lowsi punched his fist into the sand. Tony jumped in shock. – 'Now it's your turn,' ordered Lowsi.

Obediently Tony made a fist and hit into the sand. Lowsi muttered and tapped the bucket with his bamboo cane, signalling for Tony to do it again. Tony's knuckles stung as they hit the sand, but Lowsi looked at him in disgust. Once more, Lowsi slammed his own fist into the bucket and a shower of sand sprayed over Tony's face. Again Tony tried, as hard as he dared, but Lowsi slapped the bamboo cane to the ground in a rage.

Tony flinched as Lowsi grasped his arm, digging his fingers firmly into the flesh.

Again and again he thrust Tony's hands into the bucket, twisting and grinding them into the sand, one after the other. Tony gritted his teeth in pain – it was agony! When Lowsi finally released his grip, Tony's knuckles were scraped bare and bleeding.

'Continue!' Lowsi commanded. Tony knew better than to argue. He thrust his hands as hard as he could into the sand, time after time. Soon they were numb from the pain.

Tony had to do the same thing the next day. And the next . . . But after a few days his hands were becoming strong and tough. The cuts were healing over and rough calluses were replacing soft flesh. He held them out for his grandfather to inspect. Lowsi nodded slowly as he ran his bony fingers over Tony's skin.

'To be raised in the way of kung fu is a great honour,' Lowsi told him sternly. 'You will be strong and self-disciplined and able to take great pain. You will become the master of your own body.'

As he spoke Lowsi emptied the sand out of the bucket. Tony breathed a silent sigh of relief. Then, to his horror, Lowsi poured gravel into the bucket and the exercise continued. Within a couple of weeks Tony was plunging his hands into gravel and large, sharp rocks. Each time he thrust his hands into the bucket he pictured his grandfather's face. He was beginning to hate the old man and it helped him to throw all his energy into the punch. He didn't know that Lowsi's mission wasn't to earn his grandson's love; it was to earn his disciple's respect.

Each night Tony fell into bed exhausted. He might have cried, but he was too tired to even think about the pain in his body or how much he hated his grandfather. There was no time to consider what might become of him, or to wonder whether he would ever see his parents again. His body ached and his mind was exhausted with learning. Sleep consumed him in a heavy, dark cloud and, for a short time, he was safe from the horrors of the waking hours.

3

THE SHAOLIN TEMPLE

'You will wear this today,' said Jowmo. Tony looked up at his grandmother from his breakfast of noodle soup. She was holding a bright orange garment. Lowsi was busy in the other room, sharpening his tools. They could hear the familiar scraping and scratching of flint and stone. Jowmo didn't speak much when Lowsi was around, but at other times she would fill Tony's head with stories about the traditions of his Chinese ancestors. They believed in many different gods – who Tony thought sounded very unpleasant indeed – and lots of things to do in order not to break the 'luck' or 'good fortune' in the house.

'Soon we will prepare to celebrate New Year,' Jowmo told him as she swept the floor. She continued excitedly, 'It will be the Year of the Tiger.'

'The tiger?' asked Tony.

Jowmo paused from her sweeping, resting both hands on her broom.

'Legend has it that the Lord Buddha summoned all the animals to come to him before he departed from earth,' she began explaining. 'But only twelve were prepared to come to bid him farewell. As a reward he promised to name a year after each one, in the order in which they arrived.'

Tony slurped the last piece of noodle from the watery liquid, enjoying Jowmo's chatter.

'The animals quarrelled over who should arrive first,' Jowmo continued with a mischievous smile. 'Finally they decided to have a contest. The first animal to swim across the river and reach the opposite bank would be first in line to greet Lord Buddha. It was agreed. All twelve animals gathered at the riverbank and jumped in. The ox was the strongest and soon took the lead, but unknown to him the rat had jumped on his back. When the ox was about to jump ashore, ahead of the other animals, the rat jumped off his back and won the race.'

'Who came next Jowmo?' Tony laughed.

'Well, rat was first, then, of course, the ox, followed by the tiger, rabbit, dragon, snake, horse, sheep, monkey, rooster, dog . . .' Jowmo paused and began to giggle. 'The pig, who was very slow and very lazy, came last.'

Tony laughed too, imagining the pig trying to scramble up the riverbank.

'You were born in the Year of the Rooster,' Jowmo said seriously. She put down her broom and knelt down to look straight into Tony's face. 'The rooster is hard working and determined. You will not be afraid. You will be very, very brave.'

'But –

Before Tony could ask what she meant, he saw Lowsi was standing over them. He seemed able to move with the breeze and Tony never had any idea when he would appear. Tony braced himself for a beating for lingering over the meal, but instead Lowsi just picked up his cane and led him outside, through the courtyard and into the forest.

Tony trotted along behind his master, trying to keep up. They walked and walked until the trees began thinning out. Soon Tony found they were at the bottom of a huge set of deep, wide steps leading up a mountain. He looked up, but the glare of the sun was blinding and he couldn't see the top. They began climbing but Lowsi still didn't ease the pace. Tony was growing hot and weary. He soon lost count of the steps – there must have been over a hundred! At last they reached the top of the mountain, and there it was. This must be the Shaolin temple that his grandfather had talked about so often. It was a magnificent building, shimmering in yellow and gold, stretching high up to the sky in beams of sunlight. Tony shielded his eyes from the sun and squinted up at the huge pillars, ornaments and strange figures of animals and mystical beings looking down on him. He had never seen anything like it before, not even in his picture books back home.

'Come,' said Lowsi, and he led the way through a large ornate doorway into the cool of the main pavilion. There was a sweet, sugary aroma in the air. It tickled Tony's nose, making him cough. Lowsi frowned at him.

'Incense sticks and cherry blossom,' he explained. 'We use them as a gift to pay our respects to Buddha.'

Tony followed his master to the huge, gleaming statue at the far end of the temple. It was a man, sitting cross-legged, with his hands together in front of him as if in prayer. So this was Buddha?

Tony's mind flashed back to his father who taught him to pray with his hands in the same way. Dad said all good Catholic children should always say their prayers to God. There was a little rhyme they'd sometimes said together at bedtime, but Tony couldn't remember it. A lump rose in his throat as he thought about his father, but he forced it away. Memories of home were fading fast.

So was Buddha God? Tony couldn't be sure. Jowmo talked about lots of gods: the kitchen god, the god of the earth, the god of the fire, and numerous gods of the entrances and gates. In fact, if Jowmo was right, most things in the house seemed to have some god or other and she was always doing something to try to please one of them.

He looked up to Buddha's expressionless face towering above him, then watched as Lowsi put a lighted taper to a long, thin stick of incense.

'The aroma will help calm your mind,' Lowsi said sternly. 'As you follow the path to enlightenment you will become like the smoke rising from the incense to the heavenlies.'

Tony nodded dutifully, but he didn't have a clue what his master was talking about.

They moved over to a smaller side temple where Lowsi lit a candle and placed it in front of Tony.

'Now concentrate on the flame,' he said. 'Breathe deeply and slowly. In through the nose; out through the mouth.' He demonstrated and Tony tried to copy. It took a while to get the hang of it.

'Empty your mind,' said Lowsi, 'Focus on the chi and you will sense an inner peace.'

What did that mean? Tony knew better than to ask. He could not have imagined how long his grandfather would make him sit perfectly still, staring into the flame. He grew sleepy, but every time his eyelids began to drop he was jolted awake by a sharp slap to his face.

Snuffing out the flame, Lowsi finally told Tony he could move.

'Emptying your mind in this way is called "meditation",' he said. 'Only when you are able to do this will you begin the pathway to enlightenment, to true inner peace and harmony of your spirit.'

Tony frowned. It was as though his grandfather was speaking in riddles, but he didn't dare ask any questions. He had learned the hard way never to speak unless directly invited to.

'Through meditation you will learn to harness the chi,' Lowsi continued as they walked out into a courtyard. 'It is the chi that will transform your kung fu, giving you seemingly supernatural power and skill.'

Suddenly there was a noise of heavy shuffling interspersed with shouts and gasps. Tony looked across to a group of older boys, all with shaven heads and wearing orange garments like his. They were fighting one another with sharp kicks and quick strikes, but their moves were fluid, almost dance-like, and they seemed to ride the air like shadows.

'They are disciples of kung fu, training in the way of the crane,' said Lowsi. 'It is one of the traditional Shaolin systems of combat. See how they are using their hands, like the cutting of the crane's beak.'

Tony watched in amazement at the speed and power of their moves and kicks.

When they had finished, the boys filed past in a line with their heads slightly bowed. Tony couldn't help but notice how calm they seemed. Despite the speed and energy of their fighting they were hardly sweating and their breathing was steady. He also noticed the way each boy stopped and bowed low to Lowsi. Their teacher stopped too and gave the same mark of respect.

Lowsi must be really important, thought Tony. For the first time he looked at his grandfather and wondered just who he was. Tony hated him with all his heart because of the torture he put him through, yet these boys had great respect for him, as though he was somebody important.

'You too will train as they do,' said Lowsi. 'The way of the crane is just one system of combat. One of the secrets of the

Shaolin warrior is to master the many different animal imitation techniques. We will spend many hours studying animals. You will learn to become one with the mind of a beast and so adopt its ways, its strength, its cunning and means of defence and attack.'

Tony still didn't understand much of what his grandfather told him. He was confused about who his grandfather was and why he had been brought to China, but a tingle of excitement ran down his spine as he watched the boys disappear into the temple. Could he too learn to move and fight like that? Could he ride the air the way they did? What did it mean to become a Shaolin warrior? And what were the secrets that his grandfather talked about?

4

ATTACK!

Tony struggled to hang on to the excitement he had felt that day at the temple. It wasn't easy. In the days that followed Lowsi kept him busy with more and more gruelling tasks to toughen up his body to begin training. No one nursed his wounds and every day he dreaded what new challenge his grandfather would present.

When he wasn't training with Lowsi he had many tasks to complete around the small farm his grandparents kept. He remembered Jowmo's tale of the lazy pig clambering up the riverbank, as he carried another heavy bucket of pigswill. He hated the pigs – their smell, and the way they pushed, snapped and shoved at him as he tried to tip the rotting bags of leftover food into their feeding trough. He was only small and the bigger beasts snorted through their wet noses, spraying his face, and nudged him so hard that he often fell over into their stinking mess.

The hens weren't much better. They reminded him of that awful day at the airport. He could still remember the old woman, and the birds flapping about in the cage, squawking and spitting in terror.

The old carthorse was Tony's only comfort and he spent as much time as he dared in the dusky warmth of the stable. She nuzzled his face and licked his tears as though she understood something of his sadness.

'When will I be able to go home?' he used to ask her. But as the months went by he stopped asking and tears no longer came. It was better not to think about it.

The best days were when Tony went to the market with Jowmo. He found it scary but exciting at the same time. The cramped streets were buzzing with people, bicycles, pedicabs, stalls, street entertainers and vendors offering anything from dentistry to calligraphy. Sometimes Jowmo stopped at the noodle sellers. Tony's mouth watered at the delicious smells and, if Jowmo let him, he chose a steam bun with pork or, sometimes, bean curd. If she was in a really good mood she'd treat them both to a sweet deep-fried dough stick. He liked these best.

Tony stayed close to Jowmo, afraid of getting lost in the crowd. What if he was captured by one of the cackling old men and strung up for roasting like the pigs and dogs? There were lots of animals, both alive and dead. Goats, ducks, rabbits, birds, scary-looking snakes and all sorts of strange fish on a big wooden cart. Jowmo lingered, bartering with the fish-seller.

'It stinks!' Tony protested, tugging at her to be quick. As he turned his blood ran cold.

Reptile Man!

Quickly Tony spun round, trying to hide behind his grandmother. Peeping out from behind her tunic, he watched the ugly man as he'd done many times before. He might come over and grab him with his evil talons at any moment. The man spotted him and fixed him in a sinister stare, then spat at the ground and muttered under his breath.

'Jowmo, Jowmo, come . . .' Tony tugged hastily at his grandmother's arm, but she impatiently pushed him aside, unaware of his terror. Tony was sure Reptile Man was coming for him. Then, to his huge relief, he saw a young woman approach the stall and start poking at the dried snakes and lizards and live terrapins. The man cackled to himself and turned to his customer.

Tony's arms ached as he carried large bags of shopping. 'Just the medicine shop, then we will go home,' Jowmo told him as he struggled along behind her. They turned down a dark alleyway and in through a small door to a dimly lit room. An old man in a crisp white coat squinted down at Tony through tiny spectacles, reminding him of the way Reptile Man had eyed the terrapins. He muttered something to Jowmo that Tony didn't understand and she shrugged her shoulders, sighing and patting Tony lightly on his head.

As the pair became engrossed in conversation Tony gazed around the shop. It was full, floor to ceiling, of mysterious-looking jars and pots. There were huge urns, many of them sealed, but if Tony stood on tiptoe he could just about see inside. He gazed up at the shelves where glass jars of all shapes and sizes held everything from scorpions and beetles to masses of honey-bees and coiled snakes.

'Ah, you like them,' said the man, making Tony jump. He reached up and took one of the jars off the shelf so that Tony could see better. Tony screwed up his face and backed away slightly as he saw five grass snakes coiled up and floating in the clear liquid. Jowmo and the man laughed.

'Come,' said the man, beckoning Tony over to one of the large urns. Tony looked at Jowmo and she smiled and ushered him forward. The man lifted him to look over the edge, and there it was, the giant cobra. There was no liquid in this urn. It was as if . . . no! Sure enough, as he stared into the urn, the giant creature seemed to move. Tony began to tremble, but he couldn't take his eyes off the giant snake. It seemed that the whole urn was uncoil-ing, until suddenly Tony came face to face with two beady eyes staring right at him. He stifled a gasp. Sleepily, it seemed almost to smile at Tony as it tasted the air with its slithering tongue. Tony looked nervously at Jowmo and was glad when the man put him down on the floor again and the cobra returned to its coiled-up slumber.

On the way home Jowmo decided they should rest a while by a pond. It was a hot, sticky day and Tony was glad to be able to put down the heavy shopping bags. The water felt good as he splashed it over his face and neck. All was quiet and it wasn't long before Tony heard little snoring sounds from his grandmother. Sure enough, she was soon fast asleep. At first Tony lay on his back, looking up at the strange shapes the clouds made in the sky, but he soon grew restless. Leaving his grandmother and the shopping, he followed a little gravel path around the pond, picking up pebbles to skim across the water.

Suddenly he heard voices. A group of older boys was coming towards him. When they spotted him they started to laugh and call to each other. Tony couldn't make out what they were saying. He held his hand up to shield his eyes from the glare of the sun. It was hard to see them properly. Tony smiled at them, but as he did one of the boys lunged forward and slapped him across his face. Tony fell backwards.

'What? What was that for?' he stammered, trying to pick himself up.

The slap was nothing compared to what he was used to from his grandfather, but the shock of the boy's unexpected attack took his breath.

'What are you doing here, Round Eye?' demanded one of the boys, spitting in Tony's face. Tony didn't know what to say. The boys crowded round and he was suddenly very frightened.

What had he done? What were they going to do with him? He didn't answer the boy.

'See, he doesn't even speak our language,' said another. 'Get out of here, Round Eye. You've no place here, *Lo han quilo*, you little foreign devil.'

Those were the names Lowsi called him when he was giving him a beating. Tony knew that he looked different to the other boys in the village, but what had he done to deserve this?

He tried to get up, but he was pushed back to the ground. 'Come on, Round Eye, let's hear you say something,' demanded the tallest of the boys, giving Tony another, much harder, punch to the face. Tony grappled for something to say. All he could see was the shadow of the boy as he looked up into the sunlight. He tasted blood in his mouth and his head began to spin. Suddenly all the boys were upon him, kicking, punching and slapping. Tony screamed for Jowmo, but she slept on.

Then there was blackness.

✠ ✠ ✠

When Tony awoke he couldn't move. There was a humming sound and a cool breeze on his face. He tried to focus his eyes. Where was he? What was this? Soft pillows. Just for a moment he thought he was back home in London, but no, there was nothing familiar about this place. Looking for the source of the breeze he saw a ceiling fan and white walls. As he moved his head, pain shot through his body. Looking down, Tony saw that both arms and one of his legs were in large plaster casts. So that's why he couldn't move. He began to panic – and then fell back into blackness.

When Tony next came round he found the room was dimly lit. Ah yes, the hospital. There were men talking. He could only half open his eyes but was able to make out two figures standing at the foot of the bed. Tony's blood ran cold as he recognized his grandfather,

Lowsi. He snapped his eyes shut again, hoping the men hadn't noticed him waking up.

'We are sure it was the children of the Triads who attacked him,' the stranger said to Lowsi. 'They are a group from Shanghai, visiting the local family.'

There was a long pause. The room crackled with tension. Tony knew his grandfather was fingering his bamboo cane, running it through his hands and occasionally tapping it to the floor. He did that when he was angry.

'They cannot have known this boy was your disciple,' the stranger spoke again. 'They would not have brought shame to your house like this.'

'Am I to understand these boys have been dealt with?' Lowsi's voice was especially cold. Tony lay very, very still, trying to keep his breathing slow and deliberate.

'Indeed,' replied the stranger. 'The family has dealt with them most severely and the elders wish to seek your forgiveness and pardon.'

'You shall arrange a meeting,' came Lowsi's reply.

More silence, then Tony realized he was alone again.

✛   ✛   ✛

Tony didn't set eyes on Lowsi again for quite some time. He was so badly hurt that he spent many weeks in hospital. Jowmo, his grandmother, visited him sometimes, but he spent many hours alone, remembering the attack and trying to piece together snippets of conversations he had overheard.

'Who are the Triads?' he asked his nurse one day.

She looked anxiously around the room, as though she was afraid someone might be listening.

'They are the rulers,' she said hurriedly in a hushed tone. 'They are very much to be feared.'

'Like the police?'

'No. They are bad people, gangsters,' she explained nervously. 'The Triads operate all over China. But you should have no dealings with them. They respect your family. They will not harm you.'

'But they did this to me,' Tony exclaimed. 'I heard a stranger tell my grandfather.'

'The boys who attacked you didn't know who you are,' said the nurse, again looking around as though she feared for her life. 'You are the grandson of Grand Master Cheung Ling Soo. Even the Triads would not dare to offend him.'

The nurse paused and adjusted Tony's bandages, making him wince.

'I hear that they wish to make amends,' she continued.

'What do you mean?'

'If your grandfather chooses not to show mercy, there will be a bloodthirsty feud between your families for this generation and the next – until you are satisfied of revenge.'

'Revenge.' It was a word Tony didn't understand. But every night his dreams were haunted by the laughter of the boys as they laid into him. When he awoke he imagined his grandfather beating them with his bamboo cane.

One day I will be a kung fu Grand Master, he thought. Then they will be sorry!

5

LITTLE TIGER

Four years passed. Years of harsh training from Lowsi that made Tony's body strong and his mind sharp. Now he was well on the way to becoming a skilful and confident kung fu warrior. Many of the young boys in the village trained in the way of kung fu, but he alone was taught by the mighty Cheung Ling Soo.

'Why does everyone seem to know my Lowsi?' Tony asked Jowmo one day.

The grey-haired woman smiled proudly. 'Your grandfather is one of the most highly respected men in all of China,' she said. 'He is one of few Grand Masters in the ancient way of kung fu and his ancestors have preserved the art for over five generations.' She came over to Tony, tenderly taking his face in her hands. 'I know you think he is a cruel and heartless man, but he is teaching you in the highest way, the way his father and grandfather before him taught. There are no other boys in our family. Your thirteen cousins are all girls and it is important that the way of kung fu is passed down the male line. You of course . . .' Jowmo paused awkwardly, turning away.

'What, Jowmo?'

'Your grandfather finds it hard to accept you fully because you are not pure Chinese. That is why he calls you a "foreign devil" or a "round eye". Your father is Italian. We sent your mother to England for her education, but we did not expect that she would meet and marry a foreigner there. That is very hard for us to accept.'

Tony stared at the floor sadly. It was a long time since he had thought about his father. He couldn't even picture his face any more.

'Your Lowsi is a very proud man. He is putting his honour at stake, raising you in the way of kung fu. You must remember that and work very hard for him.'

Tony didn't know what to think. Memories of London had faded long ago. He didn't even think in English any more, let alone speak it. China was his home now. This was his life. His mission was to earn his grandfather's respect. It was easy to hate Lowsi for his cruelty, but honour was everything. He understood that. He would work hard and learn everything he could from Cheung Ling Soo. That way he would become the finest kung fu warrior in all of China.

✛   ✛   ✛

One day Tony and Lowsi were out walking in the forest at the foot of the mountains. The dense trees gave cool relief from the scorching sun. They often walked for hours in silent meditation, but sometimes Lowsi instructed Tony as they hiked. There was much to learn.

Today Tony was reciting what he had learned about the ancient emperors who governed China in the days before the Cultural Revolution. Suddenly he stopped.

What was that? He thought he'd heard something moving in the undergrowth, some distance away.

'Walk on,' Lowsi instructed. Tony strained his eyes and ears, hoping to pick out more movement.

'She hears us,' said Lowsi.

Of course. Tony should have known that his grandfather would also have noticed the activity. He had eyes like a hawk and could detect the smallest flap of a butterfly's wings.

'*She?*' queried Tony. 'Who? What is she?'

'The white tiger,' came Lowsi's careful reply.

Tony drew a sharp breath, trying not to let his shock and excitement show.

'She has been tracking us for almost two miles,' said Lowsi. 'You have only just noticed her?'

'Yes,' replied Tony, ashamed. His training was to be alert at all times – to expect the unexpected, always to be aware of his surroundings.

'The white tiger is very special,' said Lowsi, as they continued walking. 'Few people know she lives here. There are those who would hunt her for her coat, but she is safe in the forest.'

As they walked on Lowsi talked more of the ways of the white tiger, how she lived and moved and stalked her prey. Tony longed for her to appear, but the trees were so thick and he feared he might never set eyes on her.

'Be patient,' Lowsi instructed him. 'Keep walking. She is curious. She will come.'

Soon the forest began to thin out and Tony found himself in a small clearing. With the stealth of a lizard and skill of a monkey, Lowsi quickly scaled a large tree. Tony followed, excited at the idea that the tiger might show up. Time passed by painfully slowly. Perched comfortably beside him, Lowsi appeared calm and relaxed, but Tony knew that his senses were as alert as a bird of prey.

Suddenly Lowsi pointed his cane into the thick of the forest.

'Is it her?' asked Tony excitedly.

'Be silent and patient. I told you, she is curious, she will come.'

Tony's eyes grew wide in wonder as the exquisite beast padded out into the clearing. Raising her face to the sky, she sniffed the air. Now Tony could see quite clearly her beautiful, creamy-white fur, dressed with chocolate-coloured stripes. As she drew closer he could see her pale blue eyes and the pink of her soft nose and mouth.

'See the power in her slow walk,' whispered Lowsi. The tiger stretched out, resting back on her muscular hind legs and show-ing pointed yellow fangs as she yawned lazily.

'She is playing with us. I have tracked her for many years; she knows my scent.' Sure enough, the tiger seemed very relaxed, but Tony could feel his heart pounding in his chest as the magnificent beast flexed her razor-sharp claws.

'You must learn not only the way she moves, but the way she thinks and even the way she breathes,' whispered Lowsi.

Lowsi had introduced Tony to many animals, and he had spent hours staring at various insects and snakes as part of his kung fu training. Understanding the way they lived meant he could copy their movements. He was learning the stabbing strikes of the viper, the coiling and manoeuvring of the cobra, the cunning of the praying mantis and the stinging defence techniques of the scorpion.

The instant he laid eyes on her, Tony knew that the tiger would be his. This was the way of kung fu that he would claim for his own. He had never been so excited. He would be at one with her strength, her speed, her ability to track and hunt and not be hunted, and her sheer beauty. In mastering these Tony knew he could become a supreme kung fu warrior.

In the following weeks they tracked the white tiger many times. Tony was always anxious to complete his chores, hoping that his grandfather might take him to the forest in search of her. Sometimes Lowsi took large chunks of raw meat to lay a scent and draw her to them. One day in late summer they tracked her to the clearing where they had first met. She often went there to rest and play. Tony had learned how to move downwind so that she didn't detect him until he was quite close.

Today he led the way, with Lowsi close behind, testing his every move as always. As they came out into the clearing the tiger looked up. Beams of sunlight filtered through the trees casting golden rays onto her silky coat. She was more striking than ever and Tony shivered with excitement. She knows it's me, he thought with satisfaction as she gave a small flick of her tail and rested her head back down on the ferns. As usual, Lowsi began climbing a tree. Tony was starting to follow when Lowsi gestured that he should stay down below. What was he up to?

'Go to her,' he whispered.

Tony was stunned. What did he mean? They were already dangerously close to the wild animal. To go nearer would surely be asking for trouble. But Tony knew better than to question his grandfather. He felt his heart beginning to thud more heavily and his hands growing sticky with sweat.

'Control yourself!' hissed Lowsi. 'Focus on your breathing. She must not smell your fear.' Tony knew the technique. After hours of practice he was learning to master his own body. Through breathing and meditation he could calm his beating heart and cool his flesh. Now he focused on his grandfather's instructions.

'She knows you. Move to her like one of her own. Become like her cub.'

Tony took a few cautious steps.

'Have no fear or you will die,' came Lowsi's firm voice.

Tony was in no doubt about that! Slowly and carefully he laid down his walking stick. He bowed his head and kept his arms close to his sides. 'She mustn't see me as a threat,' he said to himself.

The tiger lifted her large head and fixed him in her stare but Tony took care not to return her gaze. Keeping his breathing slow and calm he took small, deliberate steps and edged forward. Soon he was within arm's reach of the beautiful beast. He stood for a while. The mighty tiger remained still, and then lazily let her head fall back on the ground. Tony smiled to himself.

Dare he do it? Slowly he turned back to look at his grandfather in the tree. Lowsi nodded in reassurance. Cautiously Tony bent forward, reaching out his hand. The tiger blinked sleepily and raised her face. She reminded Tony of the house cats that hung around the courtyard wanting their ears tickled. Before he fully realized what he was doing, Tony's hand was stroking her head. She nuzzled into him, pushing against his palm and showing the pink of her tongue as she licked her long whiskers. A shiver of excitement ran through him. Flushed with pleasure he again turned to look at Lowsi.

Suddenly there was a crack. The snap of a branch. Tony jumped. The tiger's head was up, a mighty front paw taking a swipe at him. Somehow Tony managed to yank himself clear, but the other paw was coming round. She was beginning to rise and Tony knew it would be moments before he was ripped to shreds! His instinct was to try to scramble away, but he would never have made it. Instead he pulled his arms back, tight to his sides, bowed his head and took a small step backwards.

'Don't move. Don't move,' he told himself, gritting his teeth. It worked. The tiger rose no further. Tony took another step backwards and the tiger settled once more to her laziness.

Tony stayed there for a while – until he was sure the beast had settled. Then, without taking his eyes off her, he walked backwards to the safety of the trees.

Lowsi greeted him with a bow. It was the first time he had given him this sign of respect.

'You're learning well,' he said. 'From now on you will be called "*Lo Fu Zai*", which means Little Tiger.'

6

KUNG FU WARRIOR

Some time later Lowsi once again led Tony deep into the forest. It was very early and they walked for miles before the morning sun started to break through the trees. Tony thought that he knew most of the paths through the forest, but today they took a new turning. On and on they walked, pushing aside stray branches, sometimes clambering over fallen tree trunks as they followed an overgrown, ancient track. Lowsi strode on purposefully. He knew exactly where he was going and Tony wondered what lay ahead. Tony was certain Lowsi had a task in mind. He shuddered. What might it be?

Suddenly Lowsi came to a halt. They had reached a small clearing in the trees. Tony gulped. Before him was a large wooden rack suspended from thick tree branches by a heavy rope. Looking more closely Tony saw hundreds of sharp metal spikes sticking straight down from underneath.

'Get under the rack in the tiger stance,' ordered Lowsi, taking hold of the rope.

Obediently Tony lowered himself onto his hands and knees, then stretched his legs back behind him, taking his weight onto his arms and toes.

'Lower!' demanded Lowsi.

Tony moved so that his thighs were parallel with the ground.

'This is called the flat tiger stance,' Lowsi said as he slowly let the rope move through his hands. The rack creaked as it was lowered nearer Tony. 'This exercise will strengthen your legs.'

Tony's face was almost on the ground. Lowsi lowered the rack still further and Tony felt the sharp spikes resting on the flesh of his shoulders, back and legs.

'Be sure you do not rise,' said Lowsi. Then there was silence. Lowsi had disappeared into the forest.

Tony couldn't move. He had no sense of time, but after what seemed like an age, he began to ache. He longed to change position, but with even the smallest shuffle he felt the sharp spikes digging into him. He squeezed his eyes shut and tried to meditate, but his arms and legs were beginning to burn as they held the weight of his body. How long would Lowsi leave him like this? Sweat began dripping from his head and face and he opened his eyes to watch the little puddles it made in the dirt.

He had to move, had to ease the agony. Ouch! He had barely shifted, but his right shoulder stung where he had jabbed it into one of the spikes. Sure enough, the dirt was now being splattered with tiny drops of blood. Tears began streaming down his face as he struggled to keep the tension in his throbbing muscles. What could he do? Nothing, just hang on, concentrate, and try to think of other things instead of the torture . . .

Suddenly he heard his grandfather's voice. Lowsi was back.

'You can relieve the ache by sweeping one leg straight across the ground,' he said coolly.

Tony's legs were in such cramp that he didn't think he could move. Taking in a huge breath he finally heaved his left leg as he pushed the air out of his lungs. A flash of pain came shooting through his body as it locked into the new position.

'This is called the bow and arrow stance,' said Lowsi. 'We will practise this and other flat stances. You must be able to change quickly from the flat tiger to the fighting cat and soon twist yourself through into the horse position.' Tony knew this meant more pain and endless hours of hard work, but he was determined. His legs were becoming knotted cords of rock-hard muscle as, every day, Lowsi introduced more exercises to test his endurance.

The next day Tony's body was still aching and sore. He was glad when Lowsi set him a very different kind of task. After their morning courtyard exercises, he presented him with an inkwell, a fine set of brass quills and a piece of parchment paper.

'You will write all that you have learned about the fighting tiger technique,' ordered Lowsi.

The courtyard had always been a place of misery and torture, but now Tony was pleased to sit there and work in the sunshine. He looked out beyond the moon gate on the far wall to the southern slopes of Hanshan Si, the Cold Mountain. He imagined the white tiger prowling through the forest, stalking her prey and taking refuge from hunters on the high peaks. He smiled. If he squinted through the sunlight he could just about make out the monastery, nestling high up the mountainside. He had been there several times with his grandfather, though it was a long, cold and treacherous walk.

Above his head the mythological beasts danced on the roof of the house. He remembered the terror of his first few days out in the courtyard. It seemed so long ago. Now he knew the meaning of these strange creatures. Jowmo had told him the stories. She, like most people in the village, was superstitious and believed that they protected the house from evil. When he was a small boy, Tony had been frightened by her strange tales of demons, gods and evil spirits. Now he knew that the way of kung fu meant he should fear nothing or no one.

Lowsi had many horrifying ways to beat any fear out of his young disciple. One was the mountain walk. They climbed for several days until they reached a terrifying ridge. A storm was raging and Tony could barely see where he was walking. He knew it would take only one wrong step and he would tumble down the mountainside to certain death. Walking was hard enough, but Lowsi made him stand at the very edge of the ridge and perform his exercises. With the lashing rain biting into his thin tunic and the gusting wind threatening to topple him into the mighty crevasse, Tony focused his mind and began to concentrate. With his grandfather standing by, there was no way Tony would show his fear.

✠   ✠   ✠

Over the next few years, Tony's arduous training continued and by the time he was eleven years old Lowsi began arranging combat opportunities. Now he could practise his fighting with other boys. They travelled to temples all over China to meet other students of kung fu. Sometimes they were away for months at a time, journeying to the north-east of the country, far west to Tibet, and sometimes across the border into Pakistan.

Tony was being trained not to show any emotion. No fear, no sadness, no joy, no excitement. Still, when he first saw the lights of Hong Kong harbour his eyes were wide with wonder. They had travelled to Hong Kong for a competition. It seemed such a foreign place. Tony had very few memories of his first home, but when he saw the men and women in western suits, the cars and the hustle and bustle, it reminded him of London. For a few moments he wondered about his parents. Were they still in London? Why had they never written to him? Was his father still ill? Would he ever see them again? Something stung deep within. Quickly he pushed the thoughts aside. What did he care? He didn't need anyone. He had his kung fu and that was all that mattered.

'The Kumatai is the ultimate competition,' Lowsi told him as he ushered Tony through a labyrinth of dark alleyways. There were lots of other men who seemed to be heading to the same place and Tony noticed only a few other boys around his age. They too were disciples who had travelled to Hong Kong with their masters to witness the Kumatai.

The air grew thicker and when Tony looked up he could barely see daylight between the tall buildings. Finally they ducked in through a small doorway.

The sudden noise took Tony by surprise. They were in a large hall that smelled of animals and stale sweat. Hundreds of chairs formed a large circle around a makeshift arena. Men were shouting, waving and whistling to get attention and place their bets. Tony and his master took their place among the frenzied crowd.

'They are bloodthirsty,' Lowsi explained as Tony gazed around. 'The Kumatai is a full-contact, freestyle competition. You will see all forms of martial arts combat today.'

'So men may die here today?' he asked, realizing that competitors would stop at nothing to ensure victory over their opponents.

'Yes, or at least get seriously injured. That is why there is so much money at stake.'

Tony looked over to where some of the competitors were warming up. There were Thai kick boxers and some using karate moves mixed with other disciplines quite different from his own kung fu. A shudder of excitement ran through Tony as he watched the frenzy of the gamblers clamouring to place their bets.

Tony knew his grandfather had fought in the Kumatai many times. He remained undefeated. He glanced at his master who was sitting in silent meditation. Then, as if reading Tony's mind, his grandfather spoke: 'One day soon, Lo Fu Zai, you will rule the Kumatai.'

Tony knew he was right.

7

SCHOOL BULLY

'You're going back to London.'

Tony couldn't believe the news. After all these years he was to be sent back to England.

'You will live with your parents,' Lowsi had announced, 'but I have arranged for you to continue your training and you will return to me when it is time.'

Time for what? Tony wondered, but he knew never to question his grandfather. Instead he tried to imagine what might lie ahead. Would he even recognize his mother and father? They were like strangers now. Would they be pleased to see him? He had long forgotten the English he spoke as a very young boy. Now he knew only Chinese. What if they didn't understand him? He had some sort of memory of being told his father was ill . . . Yes, it was all coming back now. That's what his mother had told him. That was why he was sent to China when he was only four years old. Tony shuddered, remembering the early days with his grandfather – the torturous exercises, the daily beatings.

On their way to the airport they sat in silent meditation, but Tony was troubled. He stole a glance at the old man, sitting calmly beside him. What would it be like to be free of him? Tony couldn't imagine. His training had beaten any sense of fear out of him, but something new was happening now. He had a strange feeling in the pit of his stomach and thinking about London and his parents made him break out in a sweat. Tony's world was about to be turned upside down and all he could do was to obediently accept whatever came his way.

Lowsi broke the silence only when they reached their destination. 'I have made arrangements through the International Kung Fu Federation in Geneva, Switzerland. They will approve a tutor for you in London. They will pay for the best training.'

With that, Lowsi bowed, turned and left.

Tony stood for a few moments watching his grandfather. He had always been frightened of him. More than that, he hated him. But Lowsi was his master, he respected him and he had no one else. Now he was all alone in the world . . .

The plane rose into the sky. What lies ahead? Tony wondered. What will England be like? What will my parents be like? He knew so little about them. He couldn't even speak the same language any more.

He fell asleep to the drone of the engines and when he awoke he realized the plane was landing at Heathrow Airport. The beginning of his new life. The flight attendants had looked after him very well. It was unusual for a twelve-year-old to travel alone. As he got off the plane a kind-looking woman who the airline had appointed as his guardian took his hand. He felt very silly. He couldn't remember anyone holding his hand like this, but to pull away would have been rude and disrespectful. She chatted to him, but Tony remained silent.

They followed the other passengers towards the arrivals area. Tony held tight to his little drawstring bag. He didn't have much – just another tunic and some books.

Suddenly there was a sea of faces; everybody expecting somebody. Where were his parents? How would he know them? He scanned the crowd.

People were moving quickly. They all had places to go.

'Tony?'

He turned to see two people. A woman who he instantly knew was his mother. She was Chinese. She wore bright red lipstick and had heavy black eyelashes. She was quite beautiful. Beside her a grey-looking man was sitting in a wheelchair. Was this his father? It was only when the man smiled that Tony remembered. Yes, it was his dad. But what was wrong? He looked so weak, much smaller than Tony could have imagined. The two women exchanged words, and then the guardian let go of Tony's hand, smiled at him and left.

He might have been back with his parents, but the days that followed were difficult. Tony struggled to understand what they said. His mother sometimes uttered a few instructions to him in Chinese, but they rarely had a conversation.

'I need you to come shopping,' she told him curtly one day.

They took a bus from their house to the supermarket just a short distance down the road. Tony remembered the long walks to the market with Jowmo and carrying bags of shopping. He didn't mind. It had always been good to get away from his training and join in the hustle and bustle of the little shops and the street traders.

Now Tony gripped hold of the huge metal trolley as his mother wheeled it up and down the harshly lit aisles of the supermarket. He didn't recognize most of the things on the shelves, but he was intrigued by the many colourful boxes, tins and packages.

At the checkout he helped his mother unload the trolley onto the strange conveyor belt. Before he had finished she ushered him ahead.

'Go, go. Put the things away,' she told him, waving her hand. Tony wasn't sure exactly what she was saying to him. Why doesn't she just speak to me in Chinese? he wondered feeling irritated. He glanced over to the other checkouts and saw people taking the plastic carrier bags and loading their shopping into them. Dutifully he copied.

Glancing back at his mother he noticed that she had laid her coat over some of the goods in the trolley. Now she was pushing the trolley through the checkout and taking money out of her purse, ready to pay.

'Mama, look,' Tony said, trying to get his mother's attention. She ignored him. 'Mama, you missed some. There are things still in the trolley,' he said in Chinese. Now she flashed him a glance.

'Shush!' She scowled.

'But, look, under your coat,' Tony said again in Chinese, imagining that his mother hadn't heard what he'd said. Now she fixed him with a hard stare. It was as though he was looking straight into Lowsi's eyes. Yes, he knew that look. It was the one that told him to be quiet or there would be trouble. Then it occurred to him. His mother knew exactly what she was doing. She had hidden items under her coat that she had no intention of paying for. Tony didn't know what to do. His mother was stealing! Should he try again to talk to her? Before he could make up his mind she pushed roughly past him and marched out of the shop, leaving him to follow on with the heavy bags of shopping.

They rode home in silence. Tony felt hot and uncomfortable. Why had his mother done that? He glanced up at her but quickly looked down at his knees again. She was staring straight ahead, her lips pursed together and her forehead lined with a deep scowl. He knew never to speak of this again.

Tony looked out of the window sadly. Everything here was so different. England was noisy and busy with traffic. Everyone seemed to be in a hurry. Worse than that though, his mother was a thief! I will never belong here, he thought. There was that strange feeling again in the pit of his stomach. Quickly Tony slipped into a meditation, pushing away the sense of turmoil that might easily have gripped him.

At night he slept on the floor. He couldn't get used to a comfortable bed with sheets and blankets. Often he lay awake. When he closed his eyes he imagined he could hear the babbling of the river and the noise of the crickets. But no – Canton was on the other side of the world. Now the noise of the street filled his ears. There was traffic, endless traffic noise, people shouting and sirens in the distance.

✠　✠　✠

After a few weeks Tony started at the local comprehensive school. There was so much he didn't understand and he was miserable. The other children were so rude and badly behaved. He had been raised never to speak directly to an adult unless he was invited. He could not believe the way his classmates spoke to the teachers. And why did the teachers have so little control? Why did they stand for it?

At first he tried to keep to himself. There was often a riot in the classroom as they waited for the teacher. Boys climbed on desks, shouting at one another. Sometimes a fight broke out. Tony sat in silence.

'Hey Slitty Eyes, what's up with yer?' A plump, red-faced boy plonked down on Tony's desk. Tony didn't look up.

'You don't say much do yer?' the boy persisted.

Tony still didn't look up. Calmly he ran his pencil through his hands and remembered his master's instructions. 'The art of kung fu is to keep peace. Only use your fighting skills to save you from harm.'

'Oy Chinky, don't yer know it's rude not to talk?' The boy raised his voice. Now others were watching. Tony stared straight ahead.

'Come on then, Chinks, let's hear yer.'

The classroom grew quiet. Everyone knew Steve Jenkins was a bully. He was always picking on the black and Asian kids. The others mainly avoided him, but they wanted to see how Tony reacted. This new boy never spoke. He didn't even try to make friends. What was his problem? Would he just sit there and take it from Jenkins?

Tony knew what they thought of him, but he didn't care. He didn't need anyone. As for Steve Jenkins, he could easily knock this idiot to the other side of the classroom if he chose to.

His silence infuriated the bully. Jenkins's plump face grew even redder. 'You wanna watch it mate,' Jenkins snarled. 'You better talk when I talk to yer or –'

Just then the teacher burst into the classroom. 'Places now!' he barked. The other children began lazily taking their seats.

'Steven Jenkins, get to your own desk right now!' the teacher ordered.

'I'm watching you, Slitty Eyes,' Jenkins hissed as he slouched back to his place. Stupid kid, he has no idea, thought Tony.

Jenkins continually tried to bully Tony. Whenever he saw him he shouted stupid things and called him names. Tony didn't let it bother him. He was strong and disciplined. He didn't need the hassle of a fight. Jenkins would never get the better of him like this. No one could ever get close to hurting him.

Tony was a loner. He hated school, but he worked hard and stayed out of trouble. Every evening he went to language classes to help with his English. He was learning fast, but sometimes at school he pretended he didn't understand. It was easier that way.

'One day I'm gonna 'ave yer!'

Tony looked up as Jenkins shoved his way past. Everyone was queuing up for lunch. The bully and his cronies rudely pushed in at the front. No one objected.

Just try it, thought Tony, anger rising within him. Jenkins wanted to pick a fight. Tony knew that. He also knew what Jenkins hated most was being ignored. Everything in him wanted to march up to the front of the queue and take Jenkins out. Instead he kept his eyes fixed on the floor.

Now Jenkins was looking back down the line. 'See how scared he is,' he said, in an overly loud voice. 'Too scared to even talk, eh Chinks?'

Tony's fists tightened, but still he didn't look up. Jenkins's gang laughed encouragingly. They were all longing for Tony to take the bait.

'No, not today. It won't be today,' Tony told himself.

Later that evening Tony was on his way to the language school when he spotted the bully across the other side of the street. Had Jenkins seen him? No, he didn't think so.

Quickly Tony ducked down an alleyway. Standing in the dark he thought about all the times he'd walked away from Jenkins to keep the peace. That was the way of kung fu, to keep peace and only fight as a means of defence. But now it was getting too much. Tony was angry. He knew that didn't fit with the way of kung fu either, but Steve Jenkins and his stupid friends needed teaching a lesson. Besides, he was in charge now. Lowsi wasn't there to boss him around. Tony found himself remembering the time when the Triad boys had attacked him. Then he'd been young, with no kung fu training, and unable to defend himself.

Now it was different. He clenched his fists. Next time, Steve Jenkins, next time.

'Hey, there he is, old Slitty Eyes.' Tony heard the familiar titter of the gang. He carried on walking across the playground, glancing over to where Jenkins and his cronies had surrounded one of the younger black kids. 'Off to the Chinky for yer dinner, are yer?'

Tony stopped and stood still. He didn't look directly at Jenkins, but his glance was enough for the bully to lose interest in the other kid. In the corner of his eye, Tony saw the bully slap the boy around the face before letting him go. Like a frightened rabbit, the boy fled back towards the classrooms. Anger rose inside Tony. It was one thing for Jenkins to pick on him, but seeing the young boy so terrified made his blood begin to boil. Perhaps this would be the day.

'Better be quick, eh, Slitty. The flied lice 'll be getting cold.'

Tony didn't move.

Jenkins came closer. 'What's up?'

Still nothing.

'Ah, look boys, the Chinky's too scared to talk to me. Ain't that right?' Now he stood right in front of Tony. 'Oh no, I forgot, you don't speak the English, do yer?' Jenkins started dancing around in front of Tony, pulling his eyes into narrow slits. The other boys joined in, laughing and egging him on. Jenkins came menacingly close. 'Don't yer know it's rude not to answer?'

'Leave me alone,' said Tony finally in a low voice.

It was just what Jenkins wanted. He threw his head back and let out a loud cackle. 'Weave him, boys. He told us to weave him awone,' he said, mimicking the way Tony spoke. He turned back to look at his gang, still laughing, then spun around giving Tony a sharp push.

'Hey Bosser, have you seen Chinky's mum? She's a looker. Easy too, I hear. I could show her a good time.'

That was too much. In a flash Tony responded with a round-house kick straight to Jenkins's face.

He crashed to the floor with a bloody nose. Tony stood over him and said nothing. Shaking all over, Jenkins began trying to squirm away, still on his back.

'You're a nutter, you are!' he squealed, fear showing in the whites of his eyes.

Tony turned towards the other boys. They were rooted to the spot, horror on their faces. He stepped towards them and they split and ran, like parting water.

Tony calmly walked away, leaving Jenkins to swear and curse at his deserting friends.

8

REVENGE

'Did you see that kick he did?'

'No, but Shane Lewis said he was coming out of the science block and he heard Jenkins screaming like a baby.'

'I bet he did.'

'Bosser sez there was blood everywhere. He sez he's not going to be in Jenkins's gang any more anyway.'

'Probably scared that Tony will have another go.'

'Yeah, Jenkins deserves it. Anyway, I heard that Jenkins is gonna be expelled for bullying . . .'

Tony smiled to himself as he stood outside the classroom door, listening to the other boys' excited conversation. So Jenkins might be going anyway? Good. The headmaster hadn't said much when Tony had stood before him in his office. He didn't even ask him to explain himself. Everyone, including the teachers, knew Jenkins had had it in for Tony since he'd first arrived at the school. It was just a matter of time before the two boys came to blows.

Still, everyone was surprised at just how well Tony could stick up for himself. News of his kung fu kick had spread around the school like wildfire and Tony couldn't help notice the admiring glances from the other boys. Suddenly it seemed everyone wanted to be his friend.

Tony walked into the classroom and the other boys quickly gathered round.

'Hey Tony, show us that move.'

'Yeah, come on Tony, how did you do it? Show us some more of that kung fu stuff,' insisted Simon Hobson.

Tony grinned as others joined the group. He didn't want to show off. He didn't know how to handle the attention, but something inside had changed the moment he lashed out at Jenkins. He'd kept himself to himself, quietly minding his own business, for long enough. The other kids assumed he was frightened and shy because he didn't speak good English. In fact, Tony was just sad. He was an outsider who didn't really care to belong anyway. But now he had shown something of who he really was and inside there was a sense of power that he'd never had before. Even though he'd won many victories in kung fu, he had always been at the end of his grandfather's leash, always acting only for Lowsi's honour. Now he had done something for himself. Lowsi was on the other side of the world and for the first time in his life Tony was beginning to feel strong and proud of himself.

'Can you do that thing where you smash bricks with your bare hands?' shouted one of the boys from the other side of the classroom.

'Yeah, come on Tony,' another called out.

Soon it seemed that all eyes were fixed on him. Tony's face flushed hot. What should he do? He *could* perform some tricks, but that just wasn't the way of kung fu . . .

'Hey, Sizer's coming,' one of the boys shouted and most of the other kids took to their places. Some of the tougher ones lingered, idly making their way to their seats.

'I hate that Sizer with all his standing to attention. He thinks we're in the army or something,' complained Smithy, slumping down at his desk. 'Stand up. Sit down. Silence in my classroom,' he mimicked, making the others snigger.

'Who does he think he is, anyway?' joined in Michael Leary. 'Hey, Tony, how 'bout you arrange a little meeting on his way home tonight. Bet you could show him a thing or two.' Tony smiled but said nothing as the boy pretended to do kung fu kicks.

'My old man sez we don't need that Religious Education anyway,' joined in Jason Jones, pulling a long strand of gum out of his mouth and sticking it to the desk. 'He sez religion is why all wars start.'

Just then the door opened. Despite his name, Mr Sizer wasn't a big man, but he had a lot of presence. Everyone immediately stood up at their places in silence.

'OK, gentlemen,' Mr Sizer's voice boomed. 'Today we will be studying the Ten Commandments. You may sit down.'

Tony breathed a sigh of relief. Mr Sizer had arrived just in time. He was very strict and no one dared to be rude to him or mess about like they did in many of the other classes. It wouldn't be cool to admit it, but Tony enjoyed Mr Sizer's lessons. Lowsi had taught him much about the world's religions and he was fascinated by the stories of their different gods and traditions. Still, Lowsi had always been very firm. 'There is no god but the god within,' he had told Tony again and again.

Tony had never questioned his grandfather's teaching and he enjoyed the stories Mr Sizer taught, especially those from the Bible. Some of them were hard to believe, but there was always plenty of action. Maybe one day he'd ask Mr Sizer if he could borrow a Bible to read at home. Not that there was much time for reading these days. He was still attending the language school and the International Kung Fu Federation (IKFF) had arranged for him to train at a local Martial Arts Academy. There were times when he thought about bunking off to hang around the streets with the other boys after school, but he feared such news getting back to the IKFF or, worse, to his grandfather.

✛ ✛ ✛

Mr Chang was the head instructor at the Academy. 'Ah, welcome, Lo Fu Zai, I have heard so much about you.' The little Chinese man bowed low to Tony, shifting excitedly from one foot to the other.

Tony smiled uncomfortably and returned his bow.

'Come, let me show you around my school. I think you will approve of my students.' Mr Chang placed an arm around Tony's shoulders and guided him through to a large hall where ten or more boys were practising basic moves.

'Kingsley, come and meet Lo Fu Zai, the disciple of Grand Master Cheung Ling Soo,' said Mr Chang, inviting an instructor over. Kingsley was a muscular black guy, only a little older than Tony. The boys bowed to each other.

'Please, call me Tony,' said Tony, feeling a little embarrassed. Kingsley flashed a huge smile of white teeth and grabbed his hand, shaking it enthusiastically.

'It is good to meet you my friend,' he said. Tony couldn't help but smile back.

'Kingsley is from Jamaica,' said Mr Chang. 'He is my most advanced student and I'm sure you two will become good friends.'

Tony liked Mr Chang instantly, but he wasn't used to someone from the world of kung fu being so warm and friendly. Mr Chang was jolly by nature and Tony worked hard under his encouragement and constant praise. It was very different to his grandfather's harsh training. After his classes Tony joined Kingsley, helping him to coach the younger students. Kingsley was great fun and for the first time in his life Tony had someone he could talk to. At last he had a real friend.

It wasn't long before Mr Chang also asked Tony to start teaching at the academy. It felt good being paid for his work, even though he never got to keep the money. Every evening his mother coldly held out her hand and Tony dutifully handed over his earnings. He didn't mind, he knew they had very little money to spare and he was pleased to pay his way, especially when he looked at his wheelchair-bound father. Tony learned that he was suffering from a disease that was gradually making him more frail. On some days he could barely get out of bed. Often Tony lingered at the doorway of his dad's room, wanting to go in, wanting to talk to him, but never really knowing what he would say. If only there was something I could do, he thought, sadly.

Tony fingered the new batch of notes and coins in his pocket. He felt he barely knew his father, but he would give every penny he had if it might help him get well. He imagined what it might be like to go to the park and play football with him, like the other kids did with their dads. They might go walking together, or fishing . . .

Tony heard the door open. She was home. His mother had been out shopping again. Tony struggled to understand. They had so little, and yet his mother often took a taxi to London's West End where she browsed the shops hour after hour. She always dressed up to go out and Tony rarely saw her without her bright red lipstick and heavy black eyelashes. Sometimes she came home laden with bags. 'Just a little treat,' she used to say and Tony knew that his money had been spent on more clothes or another trinket that she couldn't resist. He also remembered her stealing from the supermarket and wondered just how much of the 'shopping' she had actually paid for.

Tony listened to his mother humming happily to herself. As she began climbing the stairs he felt himself growing tense. It's just the same as when Lowsi used to appear, he thought, remembering some of the times he'd sat comfortably and at ease with Jowmo – until Lowsi's return. Sure enough, his mother's happy tune ended abruptly as she met him on the landing and Tony looked into the same steely eyes that he knew would haunt him forever.

9

STREET FIGHTER

Tony looked forward to the summer with mixed emotions. Each year, he went back to China. In the early days he used to dread seeing his grandfather. He knew the punishment would start again. Yet somehow he felt at home there. He also knew that Lowsi was the only one who could teach him new skills. Mr Chang might be a Grand Master, but in many ways Tony's skill was already far superior.

When Tony left school he went to work full-time for Mr Chang. The IKFF paid for him to travel to China and other places in Asia to take part in competitions. Lowsi was always there to meet him. Tony discovered that Lowsi bet large sums of money on him and he made sure that he never disgraced his master by losing.

'To fight in these competitions is good,' Lowsi said one day when they were on a long journey to the Jiangxi province of China. 'But the true master of kung fu must always expect the unexpected.'

Tony had heard this many times before from his grandfather, but something made him suspect that Lowsi had a specific test in mind.

It was growing dark but the air was still thick and humid. Lowsi had led Tony deep into the city where a labyrinth of alleys snaked through dark decaying slums. There was a smell of stale rice and fish. What was this place? Why had Lowsi brought him here?

It was eerily quiet and Lowsi stood close and spoke in a low tone. 'Nanchang is known for its street gangs. It is a lawless place where many have disappeared without trace. There will be trouble here, but you are Lo Fu Zai. You know how to handle yourself.'

Tony swallowed hard. His heart beat loud and hard in his chest and a rush of adrenaline slammed through his veins.

'Take off your tunic,' Lowsi suddenly ordered.

'What?' It was unlike Tony to question his grandfather, but his command came as something of a shock. Obediently Tony stripped down to his pants. What was going on? Why was Lowsi trying to humiliate him like this?

It got worse. Lowsi pulled a scroll out from his bag and pushed it at Tony.

'Put it on.'

Tony uncurled the scroll, finding that it was in two pieces joined by string at each side. His eyes flashed across the Chinese characters in horror. He had never read such foul language, such obscenities and insults.

'What is this?' he asked, sickness rising in his throat.

'You question me again?' said Lowsi angrily. He snatched the scrolls from Tony and placed them roughly over his head so they fell over him like a tunic. The words 'DEATH TO YOUR FAMILY' were displayed across his chest and he knew that far worse curses were on his back.

'Now walk,' commanded Lowsi, gesturing towards one of the darkest alleyways.

Sweat began pouring from Tony's face. He could lose his life here. He knew that. But he could not disobey his grandfather.

Crash! Tony leaped into a defence position, all senses alert, his eyes flashing. A tin can rolled out in front of him, followed by a scrawny grey creature. 'Stupid cat!' he muttered as relief surged through his body. The cat mewed indignantly, then disappeared back into the darkness.

Tony began walking, boldly now, with his head held high, senses still on full alert. An old woman was scraping the contents of her wok into the putrid-smelling gutter. Looking up, she gasped in horror as she saw Tony. Instantly she turned, stumbling in haste into her doorway, rapidly bolting the door.

Tony had no time to be ashamed.

Suddenly the air rang in a shrill war-like cry. Three, four, five, six street fighters came tearing down the alley. From both sides more were breaking out.

For a split second Tony froze. Then a great bolt of heated adrenaline shot through his veins and he was surging forward, springing into the fighting tiger position as the angry mob came hurtling straight for him.

The alleyway was dark and narrow. That was good. The street fighters could only come at Tony one at a time. The first one burst upon him with a flaying right hook. Tony immediately turned in to him, blocking the attack with his arm as he swiftly jabbed him with his right foot. The youth fell and lay in the gutter groaning. Immediately a second attacker came flying through the air with a bloodcurdling cry.

Tony anticipated the punch coming straight at his head. Ducking, he spun round, avoiding the clenched fist and knocking the attacker unconscious with a side kick to his face.

Tony's feet instinctively moved into position, ready to meet the next opponent as he lunged towards him.

Suddenly an arc of light flashed across the alleyway. A knife. He had a knife!

Its reflection bounced off the damp walls and, realizing the danger, Tony caught the thug's arm as he lunged towards him. The knife crashed to the ground, followed quickly by the howling man, grasping his twisted and dislocated arm. As he fell, Tony leaped onto his back, gaining height to launch himself into the next two attackers. Each fell easily as Tony swiftly dealt with the human whirlpool attack.

The thugs lay groaning and squirming to get away as Tony faced the final two men. Seeing the fate of their friends they hesitated to move forward.

'Come on, let's have you,' Tony said, beckoning to them with a grin.

He took a step forward, his tiger-claw hand at the ready. Both men held broken glass bottles, but seeing no fear on Tony's face, they hurled them at him and turned to flee back down the alley, cursing and swearing.

The injured men fled as fast as they could behind them and disappeared into the night.

Tony stood alone in the quiet of the alley. Even the night sky seemed to have been holding its breath. As he let his body relax, sweat began pouring from his forehead. He smiled to himself. No one could defeat Little Tiger.

Someone was behind him! He spun round, ready to strike.

It was Lowsi. The pair stood still for a moment, face to face. Tony then bowed to his master, who handed him his clothes. Nothing was said, but Tony knew his grandfather was pleased with the way he'd handled himself. He knew he was earning his respect. That was all that mattered.

THE ULTIMATE TEST

'The time has come to prepare for the ultimate challenge, my young disciple,' Lowsi told Tony as they made their way home. A shiver of anticipation ran down Tony's spine.

'Do you mean the Tar Shui?' he asked.

'Yes. Tar Shui, the "test of the tunnel". I believe you are ready.'

Tony couldn't help but grin to himself. He had heard a lot about this test. It was the one that all disciples of kung fu had to take before becoming 'masters' of their art. Whenever he met other disciples at monasteries or competitions there was always much talk and rumour about the Tar Shui among the other boys.

'Is it true that some never come out of the tunnel, Lowsi?' he asked.

'That is correct,' said Lowsi sternly. 'Only those who are truly worthy pass the test.'

Tony knew that many feared the Tar Shui, but he was confident in his skills. It would be the ultimate way to earn his grandfather's respect.

'Lo Fu Zai, kung fu master,' he whispered to himself. He liked the way it sounded. As a master he would earn not only the honour of his grandfather but also the respect of the community at large. He remembered the attack of the Triad children when he was only young, he remembered Steven Jenkins back in London, he thought of all those who had teased and taunted him about the way he looked. If only they could see him now.

Tony continued to work hard. He no longer needed his grandfather standing over him with a bamboo cane. Now he drove himself through long and arduous training routines. He trained non-stop for a minimum of five hours a day, sometimes many more. His focus was the Tar Shui and he longed for the day when he would conquer the forbidding test of the mountain tunnel.

Tony spun round, suddenly conscious that he was being watched.

'Jowmo,' he said, with a smile. The old woman had stopped her sweeping and was gazing in wonder and pride at her grandson.

'I see you are enjoying your training this morning, my son,' she said warmly.

'Yes, Lowsi is preparing me for the Tar Shui and I have pledged to work like never before until the day comes.'

Jowmo shuddered, knowing the terrible danger of this ultimate test.

'Don't worry, Jowmo,' Tony assured her. 'I am Lo Fu Zai.' He laughed confidently.

Jowmo smiled too. Was this really the frightened little boy that Lowsi had once brought to her house? She remembered the many times she had turned away, knowing that Tony was receiving some terrible beating at his master's hand. Still, that was the way of kung fu. That was the tradition of her ancestors and now she was fiercely proud of the strong young man who would continue the family's legacy to another generation.

The day came at last. Tony and Lowsi set off on the long journey north to the Shandong Province. It took three days by train and on foot, but as they reached the base of the sacred Tai Shan mountain Tony's pace quickened in excited anticipation.

He looked up at the steely grey rock and the dark opening into the cave. Lowsi fixed him in a meaningful stare as he turned to pay his respects, but nothing was said. Tony's heart thundered in his chest. Slowly he walked forward into the darkness. The chill of the mountain consumed him, like a mighty beast swallowing its prey. Ahead he could see flaming torches casting a shimmer of light on the pathway through the cave. What was that? Something on the floor was twinkling. Very carefully he took a few steps forward, straining to see. Tony smiled, recognizing the first challenge. The floor ahead was covered in vicious spikes of broken glass.

Easy, he thought, remembering the many times his grandfather had made him walk over nails, hot coals and other similar dangers. The skin of his feet was so hardened and thick that it was as though he wore rubber boots. The crane technique will do here, Tony decided. Breathing deeply, he used light bird-like steps and deftly walked over the glass, barely feeling a scratch.

Glowing with satisfaction Tony looked ahead for the next test. He had walked only a little way ahead before he saw it. The cave had narrowed and a wooden-framed structure blocked the path. Tony looked up and gulped, feeling a mixture of nervousness and excitement. Hundreds of sharp spearheads stuck down from the top of the frame. When he examined it, Tony saw that only a few bamboo canes supported the whole thing. In the middle was a maze of other canes, lying in all directions with just the narrowest of gaps between them. Tony knew that he had to climb through them, but if he shook just one the whole thing would come crashing down, bringing the spearheads on top of him.

This was a test of agility and precision. Snake movements would help him steal his way through. In his mind Tony saw the slithering python twisting and turning its coils stealthily through the undergrowth. Summoning his chi, he inched forward into the frame and began sliding his body carefully between the canes. Conscious of every movement, he manoeuvred through, arching his body and easing each limb around until, finally, he emerged on the other side. Relief swept through him.

The air was icy cold now and Tony shivered in the torchlight.

Again the cave began to narrow and soon the gentle flicker of the flames revealed the next test: the blade. Its razor-sharp edge cast tiny shafts of light onto the cave walls and Tony realized that there was something more. Of course. He should have known. The floor and walls shimmered with a coating of oil. Tony knew that they would be deadly slippery. He had no choice but to walk unsupported along the blade.

This would require the supernatural power of the chi. It was a task that could not be completed using normal human strength and skill. Over the years Tony had earned the right to the secrets of the ancient way, the way that gave him power and skill to walk the blade without being cut or maimed. He closed his eyes and slipped into meditation before stepping onto the razor edge. Very carefully he began walking . . .

Suddenly a rush of noise came from down the tunnel. A wild and frenzied dog raced towards him. 'Do not react,' he instantly told himself. He knew the dog was just a ploy to make him lose his concentration. Sure enough, a heavy chain that stopped short of the blade held the dog back. Tony stayed perfectly calm and walked on until he could carefully step back onto the floor of the cave. The dog barked and snarled as Tony eased by, smiling to himself.

Tony walked deeper into the eerie depths of the mountain. How many disciples have lost their lives in here? he wondered. How many had been driven crazy with fear? The cold walls seemed to echo with his thoughts. Tony knew his grandfather would be waiting at the other end of the tunnel. He'd heard stories about the final test that would make him a master. Tony shuddered, a mixture of excitement and terror. Would he make it out to the other side? Behind him he heard the howl and mournful whimper of the wild dog.

'I am Lo Fu Zai,' he told himself. 'I will not be defeated.' Determined, he walked on, setting his mind towards the next test.

Before long the cave widened again. Was it his imagination, or was it growing lighter? Tony drew in a large breath at what lay before him. This would take everything he had. The pathway was completely blocked by a huge slab of wood, mounted on a stone boulder. He gulped. Fierce spearheads were sticking out all over the wood, only half an inch or so apart. What was he supposed to do with this? It was completely solid. Looking more closely Tony began to sweat. He could see that the whole structure was standing on large, metal-rimmed wooden wheels. This was the key, but the wheels were thick and heavy and looked as though they were rusted into place. They've probably never been moved, he thought as he wiped his brow. But somehow I've got to push this thing out of the way.

Tony set about placing his hands so that he had a surface to push against. But no, the spearheads were too dense.

Standing back, he again slipped into a meditation, concentrating on everything his grandfather had taught him over the years. He knew he could do it. Confidently he placed his hands on the spearheads and began pushing. The spears should have cut straight through the palms, but Lowsi had trained Tony in special techniques that numbed pain. He pushed with all his might.

'Don't give up. I won't give up,' Tony chanted to himself as he paused for breath. Turning round, he leaned his back onto the spears and heaved again. The structure creaked. It was beginning to shift. Elated, he again forced himself against the harsh spikes, but now they were beginning to cut into the flesh of his back. Stepping backwards Tony shut his eyes and imagined the structure moving in his mind. With eyes still shut he again placed his open palms on spikes and summoned every ounce of concentration.

Creak, crack, creak. It was moving! Adrenaline shot through his body and at once he pushed himself against the structure for a final heave. Yes! He could feel the mighty weight almost shudder until it reluctantly gave way. Tony made just enough space to snake his way past. At the other side he let out a whoop of pleasure. He had done it!

'Don't get too excited,' he told himself. 'There may be tougher tests ahead.' He walked on. Yes, the cave was definitely growing lighter. He was nearing the end. What was that? There was a kind of acrid burning smell. So it was true. He had heard rumours about the final test. Would he be able to take the burns? Very soon Tony reached the opening of the cave. There, silhouetted in the sunlight, was Lowsi, waiting for him. Now there was one final test of strength and bravery: the burning cauldron. Tony examined it briefly, though he knew exactly what was expected of him. The heavy cauldron with glowing raised dragon emblems around its sides was red hot.

Tony lifted his head and took a few steps forward, looking directly into Lowsi's face. It was blank as usual. Tony remembered all the years he had hated his grandfather. Staring into his eyes he recalled the beatings, the punishments and the cruel training. Yes, he hated him still. But more than hate, Tony had a deep and fearful respect for his grandfather. The way of kung fu had bound them together. Now Tony shared in the mysteries of the ancient art. He was becoming one with the legacy of his ancestors. Lowsi's words rang in his head. 'You are Lo Fu Zai. You will not be defeated. You will be a master.'

Tony forced his eyes shut and summoned all his power. He felt his arms growing icy cold and numb. Then his eyes sprang open and he stared straight ahead, focusing on nothing. Tony placed his forearms on the burning-hot dragons. At once there was the smell of burning hair and flesh, but Tony felt nothing. Summoning strength up through his legs and into his upper body he forced himself to stand, lifting the mighty cauldron off the ground. In a controlled stagger he heaved it forward, out of the cave and set it down in front of Lowsi.

Tony peeled his arms from the burning urn but didn't take his eyes off his master's face. Then something happened – so rare, it quite took Tony by surprise. Lowsi smiled! His face broke and he actually smiled before bowing as a sign of respect. It didn't last for long, but it was the highest honour for Tony. Looking down he saw hot blisters beginning to form where the dragons had burned into his arms. They would brand him forever.

Lo Fu Zai was now a master in the way of kung fu.

11

UNDEFEATED

As a master, Tony now had the unspoken respect of all other martial arts disciples. He had proved himself many times in competitions where there was big money at stake. Yet he kept none of it himself. He knew that some of it was sent back to his parents in London, but every time he thought of his mother's steely, greedy eyes he hated the money even more. I will never be like that, he thought to himself.

Tony wasn't interested in fighting for money, but 'honour' was everything and he would do anything to earn Lowsi's approval. He vowed never to shame his master by being defeated, but he never knew what Lowsi next had in store for him.

One scorching hot summer they travelled to Karachi, Pakistan. Tony knew this visit was of great importance to his grandfather.

'You have heard me speak before of Ashraf Tae,' said Lowsi as the train carriage rolled through barren countryside.

'Yes, Master, I know he is a highly respected Grand Master in Karachi,' Tony replied. Lowsi snorted under his breath and ran his hands through his spindly beard.

'Ashraf and his disciples are indeed well known, but the coiling serpent is a deceiver.'

'Master?' questioned Tony, intrigued by Lowsi's obvious disapproval.

'We trained many years together as young Shaolin warriors in northern China,' Lowsi explained. 'Ashraf was a strong fighter. He mastered the art of the dragon systems, the coiling serpent and the monkey warrior.' Tony recognized the styles of kung fu that he'd studied himself.

'Did he ever beat you, Master? Tony asked carefully.

Lowsi's eyes narrowed. 'As young warriors we were as equals.'

There was a long silence. Tony shot a questioning glance at his master. Why was there such rivalry between the two men? He was dying to know, but he knew better than to question his grandfather too much.

'The secrets of the kung fu warrior are to be preserved only through the worthy,' said Lowsi after a while. His voice was low and stern as he continued. 'Ashraf Tae has opened up his school too widely. He recruits boys from local peasant families and trains them crudely. That is not the true way of kung fu.'

Tony was beginning to understand. He had been raised to believe that the way of kung fu was sacred. According to the ancient traditions, it should only be passed down through the generations by way of the most carefully chosen, nurtured and trained disciple. That was the honour he carried as the only true disciple of his grandfather, Cheung Ling Soo. Lowsi also trained some of the young monks at the local monastery, but the fullness of his knowledge, and the true secrets of the art of kung fu had been revealed only to Tony as Lowsi's chosen one.

'Then Grand Master Ashraf has brought dishonour to the way of kung fu, Master?'

'Many can train, but few should be chosen,' came his grandfather's scornful reply. 'You will see. Ashraf's disciples fight with anger and human strength. There is little art or accuracy in their moves. Their techniques leave much to be desired.'

With that Lowsi closed his eyes and slipped into meditation. Tony knew that he would hear no more on the subject. He too shut his eyes but a tingle of excitement ran down his spine. He was looking forward to meeting Grand Master Ashraf and his disciples. There would be many opportunities to show off his skills. Of that he was sure.

✞ ✞ ✞

On that visit Tony proved himself again and again, beating all Ashraf's students, even Ranni, the most accomplished.

'Now I understand,' Tony told his grandfather as they headed home. 'Ranni hardly knew how to fight. His technique was very weak; he just kept coming at me with strength, but his moves were so unrefined.'

Lowsi nodded his approval and Tony smiled to himself. At last he was beginning to understand why his grandfather had raised him in the way he had. His teaching was harsh, brutal even, but Tony knew that because of it his kung fu was of a level very few disciples ever achieve.

'Ashraf will not let this lie,' announced his grandfather, with a glint in his eye. 'There will be another competition soon.'

'But Lowsi, I have beaten Ranni. Who else is there?'

'Ranni's uncle is Adnan. He is older than you and has been training for longer. Ashraf wants us to return to Pakistan next month so that you can fight with him. He believes he will regain his honour that way.'

Tony gulped. Was it fair that he should fight against students of much more experience?

'What do you think, Master?'

Lowsi did not respond, but Tony already knew the answer.

✝   ✝   ✝

Tony stepped into the ring, keeping his eyes fixed on his master. There was a hushed rumble among the crowd. Last time he had visited the Ashraf Tae School the arena had been packed with spectators, all shouting and jeering. Now there was only a small crowd. Tony recognized some of them. They were all Grand Masters from different parts of Asia. This was a private 'closed door' fight. There would be lots of money at stake. The atmosphere was silent and electric. Adrenaline fired through Tony's veins. Although he had trained hard for the past month, this fight would be a tough one.

Adnan entered the ring. Tony fixed his eyes on his opponent. Adnan was a good deal taller than him. He wore farmer's clothes and his face was lined and weather-beaten. Tony remembered his master's advice. 'Adnan prefers bird systems. He will use the crane technique to dodge your moves. He will slip away and dance, but then strike hard from a distance.'

In his mind Tony was becoming the fighting tiger. He would use his mighty lower body strength to punch and attack with his sweeping claws.

The judge brought the two fighters together and both gave the sign of respect. Tony saw nothing but mean determination in Adnan's eyes. In a moment the fight began. Tony launched aggressively straight in as he pursued Adnan. At first, the Crane seemed to ride the air, easily avoiding the Tiger punches and snaps. They moved back and forth across the arena and the air crackled as the crowd seemed to hold its breath. Tony threw all his strength into snapping, powerful strikes, but he couldn't hit the target. The Crane danced, swooped and pranced and always managed to get away. Tony knew he could not keep this up. His strength and power was being wasted and already he was growing tired. He continued making forward strikes, but his mind was racing. What would he do? Change tactics? Yes. There was nothing else for it.

Aargh! He was blinded.

Adnan had seized the moment. He'd sensed Tony's insecurity and taken his chance. Swinging gracefully over Tony's last back fist blow, he had raked his fingers across Tony's face, catching his eyes.

Tony fought to regain focus, but already the Crane was taking full advantage. Dropping his hands to the ground Adnan swept his leg in a hard fast arc through Tony's legs. Tony felt his feet flying up as high as his chest.

Thud! As he hit the ground, the full weight of the peasant fighter came crashing down on him. Tony still couldn't see clearly, but he sensed his grandfather leaping up from his seat at the side of the ring.

This was not the end. Tony would not let his grandfather be dishonoured. He would fight to the death if necessary.

Summoning every ounce of strength, he somehow rose, but the Crane attacked again, leaving Tony breathless and with no guard. His head was spinning as Adnan's fists came whirling across his head . . . one, two, three, four . . .

'No, no, no!' Tony told himself. 'The Tiger is the supreme fighter. It will not end like this.'

Tony was dizzy and could barely see, but new determination flashed through his veins. Adnan came in for attack, but with a burst of power the mighty Tiger suddenly grasped his left forearm. Tony had a grip of steel. He squeezed. It was as though he had worked and suffered all his life for this moment. Tighter, yes tighter! Adnan let out a cry. He had not expected that. Now he was off guard. Struggling, Adnan raised his attack, but as Tony squeezed, he set about bringing the Crane to the ground. Again, Adnan yelped. He simply could not get away from Tony's clutch. Harder and harder, Tony summoned everything into the grip until, with a full-throated cry, Adnan hit the ground screaming, 'I yield, I yield!'

'Now it is over,' Tony said to himself, satisfied. He turned and bowed, giving honour to his master.

12

THE BODYGUARD

When the summer was over Tony returned to Mr Chang's school in London where he told Kingsley about his encounters in Pakistan.

'Wow, man that sounds wicked!' said Kingsley, jumping around like a puppy. Kingsley was like that. He always made Tony smile. 'That will have earned you mega brownie points with the IKFF then.'

The International Kung Fu Federation was funding Tony's training in London and helping with his travel expenses when he took part in competitions abroad.

'Well, it was a "closed door" fight,' said Tony. 'They probably won't even know about it.'

'Hey, c'mon, they're watching your every move. Chang reckons they'll want you to enter the World Championships.'

'Yeah?'

'Well it'd give the IKFF something to crow about wouldn't it?'

'Yeah, I suppose,' said Tony, a little taken aback. 'But I don't know what Lowsi would say. He thinks competitions like that are just a way of showing off. That's not the true "way" of kung fu. Many of the Grand Masters don't even go near them.'

'Tell him to think about the £10,000 prize money!' said Kingsley, digging Tony in the ribs before shooting off to take his next class.

Tony thought about the competition. Maybe Kingsley was right. He didn't need a stupid competition to prove he was the best, but all that money . . . His thoughts turned to his mum and dad. They had nothing. They were now living in a council flat in north-west London. He pictured his father, weak and frail, only able to get around in a wheelchair – £10,000 was a lot of money. Of course, a good chunk would have to go back to Lowsi in China, but there'd be plenty left for him to give to his parents. It could really help them. Maybe he should go for it.

As Kingsley predicted, the IKFF welcomed Tony's decision to enter the World Championships. They were keeping a close eye on his career and Tony knew there might be some great opportunities ahead.

✝   ✝   ✝

'Hey, here he is, the reigning Kung Fu World Champion!' Kingsley hugged Tony warmly as the two friends greeted each other. 'I heard it was no competition for the mighty Lo Fu Zai,' he said with a grin.

'Well, you heard wrong then,' laughed Tony, digging his friend in the ribs. It was a damp, rainy day in London, and as they headed for their favourite dim sum restaurant in Chinatown, Tony told his friend about the Championships.

'It was OK until the final round when I was up against Li Chang Po from Xi'an. I knew he would be tough.'

'Have you fought him before?' asked Kingsley, his eyes shining with excitement.

'Yeah, a couple of times – at temple demonstrations. He's a fine student of the Way. His master is Grand Master Gwok Siu Fong.'

'I think I've heard of him.'

'You might have. He's hugely respected. He follows the same path as my grandfather.'

'You and Li Chang Po must share a lot in common then,' said Kingsley, knowing something of the brutality of Tony's upbringing in the way of kung fu.

'Yeah. I guess that's why there's always been deep respect between us. It was an honour to fight him.'

'And an honour to beat him!' said Kingsley scraping up the last of the chilli sauce with a pork steam bun. 'So how long are you back in London?'

'Not long. I just came over for the weekend to see my folks – and you, of course,' added Tony, grinning.

'Well, you'd better call in on Chang. He really misses you at the school.'

'I know, but I couldn't turn down the IKFF, could I? They made me an offer just after I returned from the Championships in Thailand, so I flew directly to their headquarters in Switzerland to start work.'

'C'mon tell me all about it,' Kingsley said excitedly.

'Well, Geneva's lovely. They've given me my own flat and a motorbike . . .'

'What's the pay like?'

'Better than working for Chang! But mate, I'm having the time of my life. I spend most of my day in the gym teaching men and women how to fight. They're usually ex-military people who the IKFF want training up to become Close Protection personnel.'

'You mean bodyguards?'

'Exactly,' said Tony. 'They're trained in all sorts. Basic bomb disposal, protective driving, surveillance, weaponry, hostage situations, anti-terrorism, hand-to-hand combat . . .'

'Which is where you come in,' interrupted Kingsley.

'Right. I have to make sure they can look after the people they're protecting if they end up in a close combat situation without a gun.'

'Sounds exciting,' Kingsley enthused. 'Bet you've got some good mates eh?'

'Yeah, there's Jean, from Canada – he's a great guy – and Sasha. He came out of the French Foreign Legion and he's already worked in Close Protection. He's got some wicked stories . . . and Mohammed from India. They've all seen some action, but man, they party hard. They're used to serious money. I mean *really* serious. They protect some of the richest people in the world, so it's all parties, fast cars, holidays, lots of girls.'

'Really?'

'Yeah, talk about babe magnets. But boy, when they hit the clubs . . .'

'What, can't you keep up?'

Tony shook his head. 'I leave 'em to it. I need to keep a clear head for my training. I still do seven or eight hours a day on top of all the teaching.'

'You don't change do you?' laughed Kingsley.

'Well, I've got to stay on top. Actually, I'm thinking I might go for the Close Protection training myself. Y'know, get out of the gym. Become a bodyguard and get where the real action is.'

Who knew where this might take him?

✛　　✛　　✛

It was on only his first assignment as a qualified bodyguard that Tony found himself preventing a high-profile kidnapping at a lavish residence in Switzerland. For months he'd been little more than a fashion accessory and babysitter for a rich woman and her very spoilt child. He'd been bored and frustrated hanging around their fortress-style house with little to do but listen to the boy whingeing and whining. But when a gang of men had stormed the house in an attempt to kidnap the child, Tony finally saw the action he'd been hoping for. Single-handedly he'd disarmed and captured the would-be kidnappers, showing just what he could do in a hostile situation.

His months of intensive preparation had paid off. As well as combat training, surveillance tactics, protective driving, anti-terrorism, SWAT (Special Weapons & Tactics) and other essential practical skills, he had worked hard studying foreign languages, para-medicine, international criminal law, communications, and other subjects that involved seemingly endless written assignments and examinations.

Tony was soon ready to rise to the top of the game. Within a few short years he had become one of the IKFF's most high-profile bodyguards, on call to protect some of the world's most powerful men and women.

William Black was a New York businessman who always demanded, and always got, the best. When Tony was assigned to be his right-hand man he knew there might well be some action. Black wasn't in the public eye, but he'd risen to the senior ranks of a high profile multi-billion-dollar company and made a few enemies along the way. Tony had to monitor his every move. Wherever William went, Tony went too – organizing safe travel, setting up security when he stayed in hotels, even checking the kitchens in restaurants before he ate. For a while everything ran smoothly. Black was under little threat at home, but as soon as he stepped off American soil the stakes were much higher.

Tony was angry. 'One week, just one week they've given us,' he told his colleague, Henry.

'What? Another trip?'

'Yes. Saudi Arabia. It's a high stakes one as well. How are we supposed to pull that together at such short notice?'

'Have you spoken to his office about it?'

'What do you think?'

'Not interested, as usual,' said Henry, taking the itinerary from Tony.

Tony liked working with Henry. He was British but had done his training with the Gurkhas. He was older and bigger than Tony, with lots of experience. Tony knew he could trust him with his life. That was important in this job.

Tony and Henry worked late into the evening preparing a risk assessment. It didn't look good. A business deal had gone badly wrong and Black's people were sending him to Saudi to try to negotiate a deal and smooth things over.

'We're going to be like chickens in a fox's den,' said Henry, tipping back his chair to rest his feet on the desk.

'Yep,' agreed Tony. 'This is Arabian family business, the notorious Fahali brothers. They aren't happy.'

'I guess it comes down to that family honour and loss of face stuff,' said Henry.

'I know a bit about that,' muttered Tony. 'Still, we don't get a choice. If that's what he wants to do, we'll enter the fox's den with him.'

'Best get Sandra on the phone then?'

'Yeah,' said Tony, already punching out the numbers.

Sandra was their contact at head office in Switzerland. She seemed to know everything about everything. Tony knew he could trust her to do her job well and keep them as safe as possible. She would be the key, pulling information together that was essential for their trip. He put her on speakerphone and the two men went through their plans.

'OK,' she said. 'I'll get a detailed local map and a blueprint of the hotel layout. It'll show you all the exits, hidden passageways, air vents, escape routes, all the usual stuff you guys need. We have a Regional Security Officer, Abdullah Alkaff, already in place in Saudi. He'll meet you there and help you with travel and everything else.'

'I'd rather arrange the travel myself, Sandra,' said Tony cautiously.

'Hey, c'mon, trust me, this guy's OK. Leave it to us. Abdullah can get you anything you need.

'Anything?' asked Henry, joking.

'Anything from a doughnut to a guided missile.'

Tony and Henry smiled at each other, but Tony was still uncomfortable about working with a stranger.

'You can trust him,' said Sandra, sensing Tony's concern. 'He's one of us. I'll send a photo over to you, but he's a master of disguise, so don't expect to recognize him.'

'Oh great!' said Tony. 'This gets better and better.'

The next few days were full with preparations and soon they were off for their three-day trip. Henry took full advantage of the gruelling twelve-hour flight from New York catching up on sleep. But Tony couldn't rest. Something told him things weren't right. As the private jet touched down in Riyadh airport his heart began beating faster and faster. Adrenaline pumped through his body. Normally he loved the excitement of this kind of job. But this time the stakes were too high. There were too many things over which he had no control. He had a haunting feeling that something was about to go terribly wrong.

13

ARABIAN CHASE

We're like walking targets among this crowd, thought Tony, anxiously scanning the area for any sign of threat. They'd received VIP treatment on landing, drawing into the presidential slot at Riyadh airport, but Tony grew more nervous as he realized their group had to make their way through the main airport terminal building. It was mobbed with people.

Leading the way, Tony walked in front of William Black, with Henry following close behind. William was travelling with two other American colleagues, but as far as Tony and Henry were concerned, William was their main concern. They would give their lives for him if they had to.

'Baksheesh, baksheesh,' nagged a little man, trying to grab a bag from Tony's hand. Instinctively Tony shoved him hard, sending him falling into the crowd.

'Easy, Tony, easy,' rebuked William. Tony was irritated that his client seemed so relaxed. Didn't he know what danger they might be in?

'It's just their way,' William continued. 'Let's not upset the locals.'

Tony hadn't meant to be rude. He knew about baksheesh, the system that enabled the rich to give to those in need by accepting some form of help. Still, there was no room for cultural politeness.

Not today. Tony was sorry he'd offended the man, but he had only one thing on his mind – to get William to the safety of the waiting car. Come on, keep moving.

The doors swung open. There were two white Mercedes outside. Tony climbed into the back of the first one, did a quick security check and beckoned to William to get in. Henry joined them and the other two Americans got into the car behind.

'Phew-ee!' Henry whistled through his teeth as the party walked into Le Meridian hotel. It was certainly breathtaking, with its huge, glistening, white marble reception area, dripping in gold ornamentation.

'We need sunglasses to help with the glare,' William joked. Tony led the way to the luxurious penthouse suite. It would need to be fully security checked. This was a job Tony always did himself. There would almost certainly be bugs, but there might also be hidden explosives.

Finally, when Tony was satisfied, they settled William into his suite and Henry took security charge for the night. Tony knew he should get some sleep. Tomorrow could be a long day.

✠   ✠   ✠

Tony felt deeply uncomfortable about the meeting the next day. Before they met the Fahali brothers, Tony and Henry made a plan. They needed to ensure that William and Tony were never separated, so they decided he should pose as William's personal assistant. Henry was a much bigger, tougher-looking man and the Arabs would easily believe that he, rather than Tony, was the bodyguard.

Early the next morning they were driven to another hotel in the two Mercedes. The drivers followed a carefully planned route and the journey passed without incident.

'This is a safe building,' said one of the brothers, as they greeted the American guests. 'You should leave your bodyguard here. He can rest in the lounge.' Tony followed the party upstairs to an elaborate and ornate meeting room.

So far everything was going to plan.

They were served drinks and delicious sweet pastries, a local speciality. At first everyone was polite, but the negotiations quickly grew heated. A number of times one of the brothers stood up in anger causing his men to jump to attention. Tony watched them like a hawk, with his hand poised, ready to pull out his gun in an instant. He didn't like carrying a weapon. He was always more comfortable relying on his kung fu skills to get them out of a situation, but some jobs called for a gun and William had insisted he carry one on this mission.

William was beginning to sweat. The two other Americans had offered their proposals, but they could see that things weren't looking good. Now they were leaving the talking to William. Their attempt to make a new deal was obviously deeply insulting to the Arabs.

'How dare you treat my family in this way,' growled the most aggressive of the brothers, slamming his fist on the table, his heavy gold bracelets crashing onto fine, polished marble.

Tony recognized despair in his boss's face. They were getting nowhere. 'Mr Fahali, sirs, please,' William began, 'I can assure you, my company has reviewed the situation with the very best intent, but unfortunately . . .'

'You Yanks think you can get away with this,' interrupted one of the Arabs, springing to his feet. Instantly one of his men leaped to his side. 'This is not the end. This is not the end!' he yelled.

With that, he swept out of the room.

There was a moment's silence. Tony fingered the gun discreetly hidden inside his jacket. William was sitting on the edge of his seat, clearly wondering what to do next. Finally the other Fahali brother spoke. His voice was cold and menacing.

'Someone must pay for this assault on our name.'

With that, he too, left the room. Now what?

'Let's go,' said Tony, half lifting William Black from his chair and steering him towards the door. The other two Americans trotted quickly behind. Now Tony was really nervous. Were they going to be able to get out of here in one piece?

Tony was relieved to see Henry. He obviously knew that the talks had broken down. He was waiting outside by the white Mercedes. But as they neared the door, six burly-looking men with dark glasses and sharp suits closed in on them. Should Tony strike? No, not yet. He moved closer to William, pushing him forward by his elbow, towards Henry.

To Tony's relief the heavies parted to let them through, but they stood menacingly close as Tony ushered William and his team into their cars. Tony quickly checked the driver. Yes, it was the man who had driven them from the airport, Abdullah. He hoped Sandra was right, that Abdullah could be trusted. There was another man in the passenger seat. He was introduced as Omar, one of Abdullah's crew, supplied as a translator.

'Phew, that was nasty,' said William as the car began to pull away. Sweat was now pouring from his brow and he struggled free of his jacket, revealing damp patches on his blue shirt.

'It's not over yet,' Tony said, noticing that the men in dark glasses had got into a black BMW.

'Trouble?' asked Henry.

Henry and Tony could say a lot to each other just with a look. They didn't have to speak out their concerns in front of William.

Despite Sandra's assurances, neither of them fully trusted the two men in the front of their car. Henry pulled down a flap on the rear seat and wrestled to drag through a box of firearms they had earlier stashed in the boot.

Tony kept his eyes fixed on the driver and the road ahead. He didn't like being in someone else's hands like this. Meanwhile, Henry kept his eye on what was going on behind.

Suddenly Henry swore. Tony spun round. He was hardly surprised. The BMW had overtaken the white Mercedes, separating them from the other two Americans.

'Here we go,' Tony muttered to himself angrily. This would never have happened if he'd been able to choose the drivers. The best Close Protection people were trained to drive at high speed with minimum distance behind the next car, so that no other vehicle could get in between and separate them.

Tony had had his suspicions all along, but now he knew for sure there would be trouble. He watched in horror as the BMW stopped, forcing the second Mercedes to a halt. The men in dark glasses got out, walked back to the Mercedes and fired shots in through the windows at William's colleagues.

'Drive! Go, go, go!' Tony yelled, grabbing his gun and holding it to the head of the driver. Clearly terrified, the man screamed out, calling on his god, Allah, for protection. He put his foot down hard on the accelerator, but moments later he came to an emergency stop. Tony pushed the gun at him, yelling for him to keep on driving. The translator was now too terrified to speak. Suddenly the driver opened the door and flung himself out of the car, screaming, 'Allah, Allah!' as he tried to scramble away.

Had he driven them into a trap, or was he just cracking under the pressure?

Tony neither knew nor cared. He was furious. He flung himself on top of William, pushing him down behind the front seats, protecting him with his own body. Henry leaped into the driver's seat, pushed the car into gear and took off at high speed.

The black BMW was now in hot pursuit.

The dusty streets soon grew narrow and crowded with people. They had no idea where they were heading, but they'd obviously hit some kind of market. There were stalls, animals and people everywhere. Tony kept William safely out of view and fixed his eyes on the car behind. He was glad Henry was driving. Henry was one of the best in this kind of situation. If anyone could get them out of here, he could. The car weaved and spun and suddenly everything went dark. Henry swore. Tony turned to look ahead. They'd driven straight through a stall and now the fabric canopy was stuck over the windscreen.

'Hold on!' cried Henry.

He put his foot down, driving blindly on at speed. Tony heard people screaming as they scattered and leaped out of the way. In an instant the canopy fell away and they could see again. Henry expertly manoeuvred the car, avoiding people, but hitting an array of stalls, sending exotic fruit flying all over the road.

Where were they? Tony turned his attention to Omar, the translator. Terrified, he had buried his head in his hands and was muttering frantically to himself. Tony had a sinking feeling. He was going to be no good to them.

'Omar, Omar, c'mon man, tell us, where are we?'

The man just whimpered.

'Omar, we need to get out of here. Come on, think man. Get us to the embassy – American or British – we don't care. Just think!'

Omar was panicking, stuttering, and wringing his hands in terror. Tony pushed the gun at his head. He yelped.

'Here, here, take left,' he stammered, fearing for his life. Henry swung the car left, kicking up huge clouds of dust. They were in a narrow street.

'No, no,' Omar screamed. 'Not it, this not it!'

There was no going back. Henry put his foot down hard.

'Now right. Right!' screamed Omar.

The car took a ninety-degree turn out onto a main street. Tony breathed a quick sigh of relief. This was more hopeful. But then . . .

Road block!

14

DESERT STORM

Tony pushed his gun harder into the man's head. Had he led them into a trap? Henry slammed the car into reverse. They jerked backwards, then swung into another narrow, dark alleyway. Omar was now sobbing with fear. Tony knew they were getting nowhere fast. The car's wing mirrors clipped the sides of the buildings as they sped on down the alleyway. Henry didn't slow down. Soon they broke out into daylight. Another crowded street.

Tony stole a glance behind. They seemed to have lost the black BMW that had been chasing them.

'Stop the car,' he instructed Henry.

Henry pulled up sharp, grateful to take a breath.

'Get out, get out!' Tony yelled at Omar.

Terrified, the little Arab man flung open the door and hit the ground, covering his head with his arms. He thinks I'm going to shoot him, thought Tony.

'OK. Let's go,' he said to Henry and William. Then, as if to explain his actions, muttered, 'He was no good to us, I didn't trust him.'

The men drove on, finally breaking out onto a more open road. It won't be long before the Fahalis' men catch up with us, thought Tony, and we have no idea what direction we're heading in.

'We've got to ditch the car,' said Henry, as if reading his mind. 'They'll be looking for us. Anyway, we'll soon be out of fuel.'

'We need to get William out of the country as quickly as possible. They'll have all the obvious routes covered.'

'Any ideas then?' asked Henry.

'Well, I don't trust this Abdullah man, so all our Saudi contacts are no good. There's a safe house in Jordan, I know, but we must be more than 500 miles away.'

'What about Kuwait, or Bahrain?'

'Bahrain must be the nearest,' said Tony, trying to picture a map of the Middle East in his head. 'If we can get there, I'm sure Sandra can get us papers so we can get back to the US.'

Tony sat back for a moment, wondering how far they would get on foot. He looked at William Black. He was in his late forties, a pale-skinned, fair-haired man, with a little too much weight around his middle. He was quite short, but Tony had always thought he had a lot of presence, the kind that comes with wealth and power. Now he just looked scared. How long will he last in the desert? Tony wondered. He checked their supplies. Four small bottles of mineral water and a couple of chocolate bars. It wouldn't get them far, especially in the desert heat.

'Why are you slowing down, Henry?' Tony already knew the answer. Sure enough, the car began to shudder and soon ground to a halt.

Henry slapped the steering wheel in frustration. 'First rule of protective driving . . .'

'. . . always have a full tank.' Tony finished the sentence for him. 'It must've only been half full when we started.'

'If I'm guessing right, this is the main road to Harad,' said Henry, setting his mind on the task ahead.

Tony looked to his left. The land there was barren and scrub-like. To the right was desert. It stretched out as far as the eye could see, like a never-ending golden river.

'How sure are you, Henry?' he asked.

'Not sure at all, but it's my best guess. If we can get to Harad we should be able to make contact with Sandra.'

The three men pushed the car off the road. There had been little traffic, but if this were a main route to the next town it wouldn't be long before the Fahalis' men were back on their trail.

'It's going to be impossible to hide it completely,' sighed William as they heaved the vehicle into some scrub. He grabbed a bottle of water and started glugging it down. Tony snatched it off him.

'Go easy with the water. We don't know how long we'll be out here.' He was still worried about how far William would be able to walk. Outside the air-conditioned car, the heat was stifling.

'Let's leave the road,' said Henry, taking the lead. We'll head west, then turn back north to keep parallel with this road. Any sound of traffic, hit the deck, right?

'OK,' said William wearily, tying knots in his handkerchief to make a sunshade for his head.

They walked for several hours until the landscape began to change a little. At last they found shade among some larger rocks and scrub and rested for a while. William was suffering badly with the heat and Tony was growing more anxious. He knew they'd be safer travelling when it was dark, but he also knew how cold the desert became at night. The extreme temperature changes might be more than William could bear.

On and on they walked, until finally they reached a town. It was dark now and, as Tony had guessed, William was shivering with the cold. There was a sign, written in Arabic and English.

'Harad,' Tony read. 'Well done, mate,' he said, slapping Henry on the back.

The streets were quiet. There were a few groups of men standing around, chatting and smoking. They moved off quickly as the strangers approached. 'Helpful!' said William sarcastically.

'In here,' beckoned Henry, spotting a building that looked like it might be a petrol station. Inside, William rushed at a stand selling water and broke open a bottle. The astonished Arab shopkeeper jumped up from his slumber but Henry quickly passed him some dollar bills. He smiled a deep, wide smile and his eyes twinkled as he held up the notes.

'I need to use your telephone,' said Tony, making signs with his hands and speaking partly in English, partly in broken Arabic. The man stared at him and did nothing. Tony grew angry. He knew the man had understood. William came up, still glugging back the water, and opened his wallet. It was thick with notes. The Arab looked at it greedily and, without hesitation, picked up the phone from behind the counter, giving it to Tony.

'Sandra, ah, it's a relief to hear your voice.' Tony quickly told her what had happened.

'Don't worry.' You're about sixty miles from our safe house in Bahrain. Head east. I'll get false passports sorted so you can get out.'

Sandra was giving Tony coded information about a place and contact that would help them when a familiar black BMW pulled onto the forecourt. Henry grabbed William and pushed him through a back door. Tony dropped the phone and followed, yelling at them to keep running.

They fled into Harad's tiny passageways and back alleys.

There were running footsteps behind them. And shouting. Then, suddenly, a gun shot. A bullet ricocheted off the side of a building, just above Tony's head.

'Take William, keep running, don't look back,' Henry yelled to Tony, pushing him ahead. He began returning fire with his two pistols.

There was no time to think. Tony pushed William down a small alleyway.

'We're dead men,' William gasped.

'Not yet. Keep going!' Tony snapped.

More gunfire. Henry was covering them at the back. Suddenly there was a single shot, followed by a bloodcurdling cry. Was that Henry?

They had to keep going. Tony's training kicked in. There was nothing he could do. His job was to protect William Black at all costs. He had to leave his friend.

The two men ran on, pushing through doorways and hidden courtyards, climbing walls and burrowing deeper into the labyrinth-like town.

'Stop, stop. I've got to stop,' gasped William. Even in the dark Tony could tell William's face was almost purple from exertion. He was clutching his chest. 'I can't go any further, man. I'm finished. If the gunmen don't get me, a heart attack will!'

They were in a private courtyard. Tony noticed one wall had a thick covering of vine leaves. 'Here,' he said, pulling William into them until they were both hidden.

They seemed to have lost the men, but Tony knew it was only a matter of time. The men would expect them to hide in the town. He had a feeling they wouldn't find any friends here. There would be no hiding place. If they stayed here until daylight they would easily be spotted. Perhaps they should run into the desert. The men wouldn't expect that. But dare he do it? How long would they have to run? He could get an idea of direction by looking at the stars, but he had no idea how long the journey would take on foot. He could be leading William to his death.

It soon became clear that Tony had no choice. A large man stepped out into the courtyard. He was wearing a vest, and a cigarette dangled from his mouth. He'd obviously heard something in his backyard. Tony tensed. Were they hidden well enough behind the vines? William was still panting heavily. Tony held his breath. Just then William groaned and immediately the Arab man pulled back the vines. For a moment he was speechless. The men just stared at one another and Tony put his finger to his lips, pleading with his eyes for the man to be quiet.

Suddenly there was chaos. The man let out a loud cry that brought neighbours swarming out of their houses. Tony and William were trapped! Tony used his kung fu training and broke away from the man, but now there were many people milling around. It would be only minutes before the gunmen caught up with them. Tony pulled out his gun and fired it into the air. People scattered in all directions.

Tony pulled William along, again stumbling through passageways and streets until finally they saw the edge of the desert.

'Oh no!' William gasped. Then, realizing that Tony was about to take them towards the forbidding sand, he panted, 'We can't.'

'This way,' hissed Tony. 'Or do you have a better plan?' he said, pushing his boss forward.

They ran and stumbled and scrambled for what must have been an hour until Tony was confident they weren't being followed. The sand clawed at their legs, sucking them down as they gasped and wheezed their way through the dry night air. The plan was working.

'They must still be combing the village for us,' said Tony, trying to encourage William. 'When they've worked out we're not there, they'll certainly come after us, but they won't be able to drive a car into the desert.'

'How far is Bahrain?'

'You don't want to know.'

The men walked in silence as quickly as they could manage. Tony didn't want to admit how worried he was. He knew the gunmen wouldn't give up easily. They'd soon be back on their trail.

✠   ✠   ✠

'Listen!' Tony thought he heard something.

'Is it them?' asked William, terror in his voice. They turned and strained their eyes back over their tracks. There was something in the distance. 'How far away are they?'

'It's impossible to tell out here,' replied Tony. He feared there was a sandstorm brewing. The wind was already whipping up the sand so that it stung their faces and blinded their eyes. At least the storm would help cover their tracks, but would they be able to cover enough distance before daylight broke and left them exposed? He doubted it. And surely there were Arab voices getting louder, being carried by the wind? The gunmen must be nearer than they had first thought. Tony was racking his brains, trying to work out a plan, when they reached the brow of a sand dune.

William stopped. 'Look!'

Tony squinted ahead into the darkness. There were campfires. Lots of them. Tony stared, making out silhouettes of tents and animals.

'Bedouin,' he said.

'What?' asked William.

'Desert people. Come on, they're our only chance.'

Tony had read a little about the nomad people who wandered the deserts. He hoped they would offer safety. Anyway, they had no choice. They set off down the dune, towards the camp.

15

ESCAPE!

'It's a little late to be out in the desert, gentlemen.'

Tony and William could not hide their shock. The voice belonged to a tall young Bedouin man. He turned from the camels he was tending, greeting them with a broad, friendly smile. They hadn't expected him to speak English.

'What's your problem, gentlemen?' he asked, still grinning, as he looked the dishevelled and breathless pair up and down.

'We're in trouble,' Tony began, trying to sound in control. 'There are people trying to kill us.'

'Why, what have you done?'

'We've done nothing wrong,' Tony began. He didn't want to tell the young man any more and was relieved when he held up his hand, as if to say he didn't need further information.

'Come,' he said. 'You look harmless to me.' Tony took an anxious glance back into the desert, allowing the man to usher them into one of the large tents. 'Tonight you will eat, drink and rest with us.'

Tony and William were exhausted and grateful for the bread, goats' cheese, honey and spicy lentils they were served. William soon fell asleep, wrapped in a large sheepskin rug.

Tony stared into the fire and thought about his friend Henry. There was nothing he could have done to save him. He'd been killed doing his job. Everyone in this business knew the stakes but it always hurt to lose a good man.

'Good food?' The young man came and sat beside Tony. He introduced himself as Hashanni and was obviously excited to have a guest to speak English with. His language was fluent, but he had a heavy accent. He chatted endlessly as Tony's eyelids grew heavier and heavier. He struggled to stay awake, not wanting to insult his host, but he was relieved when Hashanni finally handed him a blanket.

'Rest now,' he told him. 'We will talk more tomorrow.' Hashanni was about to leave when he surprised Tony by drawing close to him. 'You told me you are in some sort of trouble,' he said in a clear but low voice. 'You can stay here for three days. My people will protect you and ask you no questions.'

'Thank you –' started Tony, but Hashanni held up his hand to silence him.

'After three days you will tell us your business, or you will leave . . .' He paused. '. . . Or we will kill you. That is the way of the Bedouin.' Hashanni smiled as he spoke, but something told Tony he was deadly serious.

'Thank you for your generous hospitality,' said Tony, giving a bow.

Hashanni laughed out loud, clapping his hands in delight.

To his surprise, Tony slept soundly that night.

✠   ✠   ✠

The next day William and Tony stayed close to Hashanni. Tony guessed that no one else in the Bedouin camp spoke English. They didn't show much interest in the foreigners anyway. Hashanni busied himself tending to the camels, which Tony eyed suspiciously. He'd studied many animals during his kung fu training but the camel remained a mystery. There was something he didn't like about them.

'She's got her eye on you,' joked William as the two of them watched Hashanni prepare nosebags of food.

'What's in this stuff, anyway?' asked Tony, reaching out to one of the bags. Before he knew what was happening, one of the beasts came lunging towards him, spitting and snorting.

'Hey, get away, shoo, shoo!' Tony cried as the camel started to snap, trying to bite him. He backed away, but the camel had a determined look in her eye. He turned to run. The camel followed in hot pursuit.

'Do something!' Tony yelled to Hashanni, but all he could hear was William and the young Bedouin laughing. Even some of the other tribespeople had stopped what they were doing. They could not help but laugh at the commotion.

Tony headed for the nearest tent and dived in. Outside he could hear the camel snorting and hoofing the dust, waiting for him to come out.

'It's OK, my friend.' It was Hashanni. 'You can come out now. I have her on a chain. She thought you were going to take her food.'

Tony tentatively poked his head out of the tent. The camel was tethered close by with her nose buried in her nosebag. He eyed her warily and she stopped eating for a moment, snorting her disgust.

William caught up with them, wiping tears of laughter from his eyes. He seemed a completely different person from last night's cowed fugitive.

'Oh yes, very funny!' said Tony irritated. He hated being made to look a fool.

'C'mon Tony, lighten up. You gotta see the funny side,' said William, still choking with laughter.

Hashanni patted Tony on the back. 'Don't worry, my friend. This afternoon I will teach you to ride.'

Tony smiled weakly. He had no desire to learn to ride the horrid beast, but something told him this might be their only way out of the desert.

✠   ✠   ✠

Tony and William stayed with the Bedouin for two days until they were more rested.

'You remind me of Lawrence of Arabia,' laughed William as he watched Hashanni help Tony onto a hostile-looking camel.

'Who?' asked Tony, not really caring anyway. He'd had to swallow a lot of pride to even go near the beast again and he certainly didn't trust her. The feeling was obviously mutual. The camel snorted haughtily and refused to budge when Tony tried to get her to walk. He copied the strange guttural noise Hashanni made and flapped the reins, but the camel stubbornly dug her hooves into the ground.

'She's going nowhere, buddy,' laughed William, but before Tony could answer back Hashanni whipped the camel's flanks, setting her off at a furious canter that had Tony clinging on for his life.

Tony was intrigued by the Bedouin people. They were quiet and deeply religious, giving thanks to Allah before every meal and keeping the Muslim law of prayer five times a day. Inside their tents Tony marvelled at the sight of men, women and children methodically working in silence at intricate and colourful weavings. 'We will sell these and other crafts when we next visit a town,' Hashanni explained, proudly introducing the foreigners to the fine artistry of his people.

Hashanni was a great host, but Tony could not forget the three-day deadline. He didn't want to get into deeper water and he was anxious to get his boss back to America as soon as possible. A couple of hundred dollars secured them a camel each and they headed off into the desert, towards Qatar.

'When you get there this man will help you get to Bahrain,' Hashanni had told them. He'd pushed a piece of paper into Tony's hand with a name and address. 'Tell him Hashanni of the Bedouin sent you. He will keep you safe.'

'Thank you,' said William, slipping Hashanni a roll of notes. 'We are indebted to you.'

'Travel safely, my foreign friends.'

Sure enough, it wasn't long before Tony and William were aboard a packed boat to Bahrain. It was hot and smelly, and there were many animals pushing and shoving among the people.

'Now I know why I prefer to fly,' said William.

✠   ✠   ✠

They'd made contact with Sandra at head office and she'd arranged for a German, Julian, to meet them from the boat.

'New papers,' he explained, handing each man an envelope.

Tony looked at his new passport and smiled. 'Ah, so now I'm an Italian, Antonio Carreras.'

'You speak Italian, right?' asked Julian.

'Well enough to get by – I'm half Italian. Don't worry, we'll keep our mouths shut and we shouldn't have any trouble,' said Tony.

'Just as well,' interrupted William, 'because I don't speak a word of Dutch.' He showed Tony his fake passport.

Tony laughed. 'Walter Schmidt of the Netherlands. Yeah, it suits you!'

'You've also got airline tickets in there,' said Julian. 'Bulgarian Airlines. It won't be a direct route home, but we didn't want you to take a US airline in case the Fahalis have them covered.'

'Sure,' said Tony. 'I know the deal.' He knew it was too soon to relax, but couldn't help breathing a sigh of relief when they took off from Bahrain, and the next day he gave a silent cheer when they finally touched down at JFK airport, New York.

William rewarded him handsomely. 'I owe you my life,' he told him.

'It's what I'm trained to do, sir.' Tony smiled. 'Still, I'll be happy never to set foot in Saudi Arabia again.'

A few days later Tony was sent details of his next assignment. 'No!' he exclaimed, laughing in disbelief. He was to become right-hand man to Amin Fahed the Saudi Arabian ambassador to the UK, Italy and Cyprus!

16

LOVE AT LAST

Tony travelled the world with Amin Fahed. His government wanted the best protection for their ambassador. He headed up a five-man elite security team and enjoyed the high life as Fahed moved between his luxury houses in London, Naples in Italy and Limassol in Cyprus.

Tony was very well paid, but he didn't have much time to spend his money. He didn't need to anyway. Instead he sent a lot of it back to his parents, setting them up in a fine apartment in Paddington, London. At last his mother had the wealth she had always dreamed of. Tony was happy he could provide for his parents, but he tried not to think about them too much. Despite his generosity his mother never seemed pleased to see him. She was still cold. It's like she doesn't know how to behave around me, even after all these years, Tony thought sadly.

All his life Tony had pushed certain thoughts from his head. 'Why couldn't he have been raised like a normal child? Why were his parents so uncaring? What had he done to deserve this? Sometimes these questions haunted his dreams. He re-lived the scenes of being sent away to China as a small boy, his grand-father's beatings, meeting his parents as though they were strangers, the bullies at school . . . He often woke in the middle of the night, sweating and moaning. Wiping his brow he would look in the mirror to remind himself where he was, who he was.

'I am strong and successful. I need no one,' Tony told himself. 'I am Amin Fahed's right-hand man and I have a job to do.' With that he would begin to meditate and perform the ancient exercises of the kung fu master. He remembered the Tar Shui and the day he emerged from the Tai Shan Mountain, proudly carrying the burning hot dragon cauldron. He thought about his grandfather. Growing up he'd hated him for his cruelty, but somehow he was driven to please him, to earn his respect. Only then could he be happy. Lowsi's words rang in his ears, 'Lo Fu Zai, always remain undefeated.'

✠   ✠   ✠

'Hey, Gerry,' how's it going?' Tony greeted the young Chinese man with a warm handshake. He didn't have many friends, but when he was in London Tony often hooked up with Kingsley or one of the old students from Mr Chang's school. He was on a two-week break while Amin Fahed went back to Saudi Arabia and had decided to spend time with his parents.

It was a beautiful summer day and Tony and his friend had hired a boat on the lake in London's Hyde Park. There were lots of people enjoying the sunshine and the place was packed with students and tourists having a great time on the water. Gerry rowed lazily around and Tony lay back enjoying the warmth on his face.

'Hey, Tony, check this out,' said Gerry, giggling. Tony sat up, squinting through the sunlight. Just ahead there were three blonde girls in a boat. They had lost one of their oars and two of them were hanging over the side of the boat, trying to reach it. Tony and Gerry watched. The girls were giggling and splashing about so much that the boat tipped and bobbed as it moved backwards, away from the stray oar.

'Need any help?' Tony shouted. Gerry was already rowing towards the girls.

'Ah, knights in shining armour,' one of the girls exclaimed as they drew alongside. Tony knew he could easily get the oar for them, but it would be much more fun to 'rescue' the girls properly.

'There's no way that'll be any good to you,' he laughed as the oar floated away. 'You'd better jump into our boat and we'll take you ashore.'

The girls giggled some more and spoke hurriedly amongst themselves before agreeing to the plan. They introduced themselves first. 'I am Leah,' said the taller girl, 'and these are my sisters Lena and Aiya. We're from Sweden.'

Gerry introduced both himself and Tony as he took Leah's hand, helping her into their boat. Both vessels rocked dangerously as she clambered aboard amid more laughter. Once she felt safe, Leah turned and held out her hand to her sister. 'Aiya, reach out, here's my hand.'

Tony looked at the younger girl who was crouching in the boat, clinging nervously to the side. He noticed the other sister Lena helping her up, as though she could not manage herself. It was then that it struck him. She's blind, he realized.

The girl stood up and leaned towards Leah, but as the boat rocked Leah stumbled backwards with a squeal, landing on Gerry. With Leah's hand gone from her reach, Aiya was beginning to fall but, just in time, Tony caught her by her waist, lifted her high out of her boat and set her gently down in his. For a moment he held her – until he was sure she'd got her balance. With his face close to hers, Tony saw brilliant blue eyes and a beautiful smile.

Something was happening. A tingle ran through Tony's body, leaving him strangely breathless. It was for just a fleeting moment, and then Tony remembered the other girl left in the boat. He held out his hand, only to find Gerry was already there.

Tony and Gerry took an oar each and rowed the sisters back to shore.

'We are so grateful to you,' giggled Leah. 'You must let us buy you a coffee and some cake by way of thanks.'

The boys didn't need much persuading. As they moored the overloaded boat Leah, Gerry and Lena jumped ashore and Tony stood back beside Aiya. He didn't know how best to help her. He positioned himself ready to lift her, as he did his father when helping him into his wheelchair. Sensing his insecurity, Aiya giggled. Gently she guided Tony in front of her so that she could rest her right hand on his shoulder.

'Now that will be fine,' she said, gesturing that he should step out of the boat. Using Tony as a guide, Aiya was able to step confidently onto the lakeside.

Tony found himself strangely breathless again. Aiya's hand did not leave his shoulder while she moved around to face him. She reached up her left hand and started gently touching his face, running her fingers over his forehead, his eyes, down his nose, across his cheeks and chin. She was *seeing* him with her hands.

'Hmmm, you're really good-looking,' she said mischievously. Tony blushed, but he grinned from ear to ear.

'Are you flirting with me?' he asked.

As the afternoon wore on Tony found himself unable to take his eyes off Aiya. She was beautiful and such good fun. 'She's the clever one,' Leah said, noticing the way Tony was watching Aiya. 'Did she tell you she's living in London studying law? We're just visiting tourists,' she smiled, winking at Lena. Tony blushed again. Might he have the guts to invite Aiya out with him? He wondered what her sisters might think, but he needn't have worried . . .

'It's fabulous here!' enthused Aiya later that evening as Tony guided her through London's Chinatown.

'I knew you'd love it,' said Tony, delighted to watch Aiya drinking in the atmosphere of the streets. It was a warm, balmy evening and people were staying out late. Delicious smells floated out of the restaurants and the chatter of Cantonese and Mandarin dialects filled the air.

After that, Tony and Aiya visited Chinatown many times. It was the beginning of a very special friendship.

Tony loved his work and travelling with Amin Fahed, but now he found it harder to leave London. He flew back to see Aiya whenever he could. They talked for hour after hour, walking in London's parks or taking boat trips on the Thames. The evenings saw them in Chinatown or at a cinema, where Tony would whisper descriptions of the film scenes into Aiya's ear, often making her giggle. At the end of each term she went back to Sweden and Tony was sometimes able to join her at the family home.

✝   ✝   ✝

One night, back in Italy, Tony lay awake thinking. He checked the clock. It was midnight. London was one hour behind, but he guessed Aiya might still be studying. Thinking about her made his face break out in a smile. She was beautiful, clever and funny. He never laughed so much as he did when he was with her. She had a wonderful family too. That's where she gets her confidence from, thought Tony with a smile. It made him think about his own family. He never spoke much about his parents and the sadness he felt inside, but somehow Aiya seemed to understand.

'You are lonely,' she had told him soon after they first met.

'Lonely?' he'd answered in surprise. He'd never really thought about it before, but yes, maybe that was it? Lowsi's training had made him strong and disciplined. He really believed he didn't *need* anyone, but sometimes, alone with his thoughts, he had to admit he felt deeply sad and somehow lost.

'Don't worry,' Aiya had said, her eyes twinkling. 'You've got me now, you can be happy.' She'd smiled mischievously, making Tony feel something new and strange, something he liked very much.

17

TORN APART

Tony didn't like being away from Aiya, but she was studying hard and he had work to do in Cyprus. When Amin Fahed based himself in Cyprus, Tony stayed in an apartment owned by the IKFF, which he was now sharing with a couple of professional basketball players. Like Tony, they were highly disciplined sportsmen who took their training very seriously. Still, William and Kevin were great fun, and when he wasn't working Tony enjoyed hanging around the apartment with them, joining in their wisecracks and pranks. William was the worst. He was a huge guy from Chicago who always had some kind of joke up his sleeve.

Tony and William were engrossed in a film late one night when the telephone rang. At first they both ignored it, but eventually William uncurled his long legs from the sofa and went to answer. Tony barely noticed him move.

Moments later William came back and stood in front of him.

'What? Man, get out of the way of the TV,' Tony protested. His friend turned and switched it off.

'Tony, mate, there's really bad news. She's dead! Aiya's been killed in a car accident . . .'

In that moment Tony's world came crashing down.

William told him that Aiya had been out with a friend in London. Some joyriders, high on drink and drugs, had overtaken a lorry in a stolen car and crashed headlong into the girls' car. Everyone was dead.

Tony's lungs felt as though they were about to burst. He gasped for air, his heart thundered in his chest. Something mad and uncontrollable shot through his veins and he lashed out at William.

'What, is this one of your sick jokes?' he screamed. Rage flared up within him and he pinned the huge man to the floor, yelling, 'I don't believe you, I don't believe you.'

But deep down Tony knew that even William wouldn't joke about something like this. It was true. Aiya, his best friend, the only person he'd ever loved, was gone. Dead. Nothing would bring her back.

✛   ✛   ✛

From that moment something changed inside Tony. Nothing would ever be the same again. The anger that raged inside him on the night of Aiya's death was like a deadly poison and it festered and grew until it overwhelmed him. All the hatred that had built up during his early life had never gone away. It had just been lying dormant. Tony's successes and self-control and, of course, Aiya had helped subdue it, but now at last it was being unleashed like an ugly beast, ready to attack anyone.

Everyone around him could see Tony was out of control. William and Kevin tried to help, to talk to him, but he threatened to beat them up. He didn't want anyone's sympathy. He just wanted to be left alone. The IKFF instructed him to take a break, but Amin Fahed contacted him directly. He was due to leave on another trip and wanted Tony with him. Tony was anxious to get back to work. Perhaps if he kept himself busy it would help him forget about what had happened. But Tony couldn't forget. All he could think about was Aiya and the lunatics who had taken her away from him. A deep and deadly rage was brewing in his heart.

✠ ✠ ✠

'What happened to you? Amin asked with a smirk one day. He had noticed the deep bruising above Tony's eye.

'Just a bar brawl, nothing I couldn't handle,' muttered Tony, embarrassed at having to explain himself to his boss. But the previous evening his only emotion had been excitement. He'd needed to fight and some drunken sailors had been the ideal – and unlucky – opponents.

'Tonight is playtime. I want you with me at the casino,' Amin said. The Arab blew cigar smoke into the air and grinned widely, flashing several gold teeth. He went to the safe and pulled out thick bundles of banknotes, each secured with a gold clip. 'I have a good feeling about tonight,' he said with a wink.

The casino was busy and everyone greeted Amin with a handshake or a respectful bow as they were escorted through to the private lounge. As right-hand man, Tony was to remain close to Amin at all times. The rest of the team would cover various other points in the building. Amin had many enemies, so he never went anywhere without his Close Protection unit.

The manager escorted Amin to his favourite table and Tony recognized the familiar self-assured pleasure fall over Amin's face as he was dealt the cards. The game was beginning when a rather sweaty little man appeared at Amin's side. Speaking hurriedly to Amin, he pawed at him like a pleading puppy dog. Tony watched like a hawk. Amin was getting irritated. Tony waited. When Amin gave the nod Tony stepped forward, very close to the man, giving him a clear signal that he should leave. The man hesitated. Frightened, he looked at Tony, but then carried on talking, faster and more desperately. Tony didn't wait for another sign from Amin. He simply kicked the man in the throat. Yelping, he scampered away like a frightened rabbit. There was a gasp among the other players and the room fell silent.

Amin clapped his hands. 'Gentlemen, shall we play?' he said in his deep, resonating voice. Everyone carried on as though nothing had happened. A moment later Amin caught Tony's eye and nodded at him in approval.

The next day Tony was summoned to Amin's private penthouse.

'Excellent work last night, Tony,' he said, wringing his hands in pleasure. 'Excellent. You are a loyal and highly valued member of my team. Amin sat behind his marble and rosewood desk, picking at his gums with a toothpick. In front of him were the previous night's winnings. Amin always liked to count his own cash. He caressed it as though it were a prize cat. Bundles were piled high.

There must be thousands and thousands of dollars just on this table, thought Tony. He knew what Amin was about to ask him. Once before, Tony had politely turned down Amin's request to collect a debt for him. Amin had wanted him to beat up the man who owed him money, and as far as Tony was concerned this was way beyond the call of duty. Things were different now. He knew that this time he was going to accept the job, but it had little to do with money.

In the space of only a few weeks Tony had become a very different man. The self-controlled, highly disciplined disciple of martial arts had morphed into an angry and bitter young man, full of aggression and hatred. The only thing that helped him to feel better was letting out his rage in a fight. It was a dangerous and horrible situation.

So Tony began collecting debts for his boss. He always got the money and always left a beating. Amin was delighted.

18

DOWNWARD SPIRAL

Tony was out of control. Weeks went by and he spiralled deeper and deeper into a vortex of violence and hatred. When he wasn't working Tony spent his time in the bars around Limassol. It wasn't that he wanted to get drunk (he drank only milk or orange juice). Tony had been raised not to touch alcohol – it didn't suit the disciplines of the way of kung fu.

The 'way' of kung fu . . . Tony found himself thinking about what it really meant. It was everything. Yes, it was everything that Tony was, it was all he had ever strived for . . . but now, without Aiya, nothing mattered any more. It was all meaningless and empty. He'd been devoting less and less time to the training and meditation that had been so much part of his life; meditation required peace and there was no peace within him. These days his mind was in permanent turmoil, always racing, always looking for the next fight. He couldn't bear to be alone, but his friends had long since abandoned him. They were frightened of him.

✝   ✝   ✝

'Tony, it's me, your mother.'

Tony scrambled to pull himself together, glancing at the clock on the wall. It was nine in the morning, only a few hours since he'd returned and fallen asleep on the sofa. He was still fully clothed, with a half-smoked cigarette twisted between his fingers. He was dreaming. The phone was ringing. That was his recurring nightmare. The ringing phone bringing terrible news . . .

But this was real. He really had picked up the phone and now his mother's voice was coming at him, cold and clear.

'Tony, are you there?'

'Yes, yes, I'm here,' he managed groggily.

'Tony, there's great news.' Tony had rarely heard his mother sounding excited. It threw him back to a childhood memory from before he was sent to China. His father was fit and well then and working as a successful electronics engineer. That day his father had burst in through the door, excitedly throwing money into the air. He'd been paid in cash from a private customer. In his mind's eye Tony saw his mother rushing to embrace his father. They had danced around the room together, whooping in delight, his father lifting his mother high into the air until they'd both collapsed in fits of laughter. Tony hadn't understood what was going on, but now the memories came flooding back. It was one of so few happy memories.

'Tony?'

'Yes. News, what news?' he said, brushing cigarette ash off his clothes.

'There might be some treatment for your father. Some doctors in Switzerland are doing trials on people with your father's illness. They've had some success. Tony, he's getting very ill, he really needs this.'

Tony struggled to take in what his mother was telling him. He wasn't used to phone calls from his parents and was still in shock.

'Tony, we need £30,000 –' she paused.

'For the treatment?' Tony asked.

'Yes, and so we can stay in Switzerland.'

This irritated Tony. How much money did she think he had? He gave a big chunk of his earnings to his parents anyway. But when he thought of his father, he knew he had to help.

'Don't worry, Mother. I'll get the money.'

Later that morning Tony paced the floor in the apartment. It was such a lot of money. He was well paid, but he had no savings and he'd never be able to raise that much easily. Amin could help, but Tony had too much pride to ask. He didn't want to be in debt to anyone. Still, there might be a way . . . Adrenaline began running hot and fast through his body. Yes, he knew what he must do.

The next time Amin asked Tony to collect a debt he collected a little more and kept it for himself. After that he grew more confident. It was so easy. Then he began robbing hotel rooms. He picked the most expensive hotel in town and walked in confidently, posing as a guest. Most people went out for the evening so it was easy to break in quietly and ransack their rooms. People had a lot of cash with them on holiday and there were rich pickings.

Tony arranged for his parents to fly out to Cyprus so he could give them the money they needed. They stayed for a short break at his apartment and he showed them around the island. Still, they weren't used to family holidays together and Tony was glad when it was time to take them back to the airport. He couldn't help feeling irritated and angry, though he tried not to show it. They'd never asked how he was, and never even mentioned Aiya's name. It was as though she had never existed.

He left them at the airport and drove back to town like a madman. Tony often drove too fast these days, especially when he was out on his motorbike. There had been several near accidents, but he didn't care. Sometimes he thought it would be better if he just drove his bike over the side of a mountain. The police often chased him, but if they ever caught up he showed them his identity card. Because Tony worked for a diplomat he could get away with breaking the speed limit.

Amin didn't need him to work that night, but Tony couldn't face going home. The twinkling lights of Limassol stretched out before him and he wanted company.

He chose a table and sat down with his coffee, watching the people go by. Limassol was lively with tourists and local people taking an evening stroll. He tried not to think too much. Eventually Kevin, one of the basketball players, came over.

'Hi Tony, I thought it was you,' he said tentatively. Tony rose to greet him warmly. Kevin was relieved. You never knew what kind of mood Tony might be in these days.

'Please, come and join me,' said Tony, pulling out a chair. He was pleased for the company, but he knew what Kevin must have been thinking. 'It's really good to see you. I'm sorry, I know it's been a while.' he said, calling the waiter over to take Kevin's order.

After a while a group of young English people arrived in the square and set up a large wooden cross, just a little way from where Tony and Kevin were sitting.

'Oh no, Bible-bashers,' said Kevin. 'I think we're about to hear a sermon.' Tony just smiled and sipped his coffee. As they watched, a small crowd gathered and the young people began playing guitars and singing songs. Some tourists walked by, jeering and shouting insults.

'There's no need for that is there? They're not doing anyone any harm,' Tony said, annoyed to see a bunch of British youths shouting and heckling above the singing as they passed by.

'I guess they're used to it,' said Kevin, laughing. 'Come on, let's go somewhere else. The guys are meeting at the Afrikana.'

Kevin threw a few coins down on the table and stood to leave.

'No, you go ahead,' Tony said. He didn't feel like a club and for the first time in ages he felt relaxed. He realized he was quite enjoying watching the spectacle. He signalled to the waiter for another coffee and turned his attention back to the 'Bible-bashers'.

After a while the group put the guitars down and one of the young men started to address the crowd.

'Who wants this bottle of wine?' he asked. He called out several times, catching the attention of a few more passers-by who stopped to listen. 'Come on, who wants it? It's free . . . there's no catch.'

By now there was a crowd of about twenty people, all intrigued. At first no one took the bottle, but eventually a woman stepped forward.

'I'll have it,' she said, stretching out her hand. The crowd watched expectantly as the man handed her the bottle. She hesitated, and then took it.

'Thank you,' she said, returning to her friends.

The young man continued speaking to the crowd. Now he really had their attention. He was about the same age as Tony, with longish hair, dressed in a T-shirt and Bermuda shorts. He spoke with a familiar accent and Tony guessed he might be from London. Probably a student, thought Tony.

'See,' the young man said, gesturing towards the woman – now hugging her bottle of wine, 'No strings attached. As I promised, it's a present, completely free. All you have to do is step forward and take it.' The crowd listened expectantly.

'This is just like Jesus' gift of salvation,' the preacher continued. 'Jesus loves every single person in the world and his gift of life is free. All we have to do is take it. God is not a God who will force anything on us. It's up to us to step forward.'

God. Which god? Tony smirked, remembering Jowmo fussing around, trying to please all her gods. Then his grandfather's words rang around his head: 'There is no god, but the god within.' Yes, that's what he believed. Through kung fu he'd learned to harness the chi and it seemed to give him a kind of super power. 'I don't need anything from any god', Tony told himself. 'I am in charge of my own life. And I am strong – because I make myself that way.'

'Salvation is the greatest gift ever given . . .' the preacher's words broke through again. What was this salvation thing he was talking about? Now Tony remembered his RE teacher, Mr Sizer, and yes, he could remember a whole lesson on the 'salvation' idea. Tony closed his eyes and could see Mr Sizer writing 'Forgiveness' in great big letters on the blackboard. He had paced around the classroom, thirty pairs of eyes not daring to stray from him.

'Imagine wiping away all the bad things you have done in life. Imagine them all being forgotten so that you can be clean before God. Christians believe that this is what happens when they follow Jesus. They are saved by believing in him,' Mr Sizer had taught them.

Tony felt suddenly sad but, for once, it wasn't anything to do with memories of Aiya, or of Mr Sizer or of his school days. He was thinking about some of the terrible things he had done in the last few weeks, the people he'd hurt, and the money he'd stolen. I don't think I could ever be clean before any god, he thought.

Quickly he pushed the thoughts aside. Careful Tony, don't get miserable, he warned himself. The guitars were playing again. Tony took a deep drink of thick black coffee.

19

TROUBLE

'Mind if I join you?'

Tony looked up from his drink. It was the young preacher standing there.

Tony hesitated but pulled out a chair.

'Sure,' he said, wondering if this was a good idea.

'I noticed you sitting here all the time. What did you think?' Tony didn't really know what to say.

'Yeah, nice little show, I guess. Good crowd,' he said, smiling and surprising himself. It was in his nature to be wary and suspicious of people.

'I'm Martin,' the man said. Tony was relieved he hadn't offered a handshake. He hated people being over-friendly.

'I'm Tony.'

Martin ordered a lemonade and chatted as his friends packed up the guitars and talked with other passers-by.

'We're over working with a local church for the summer,' he explained. 'It's been great fun so far. We've been on the beach a lot and done this kind of thing most evenings. Cyprus is a beautiful place, isn't it?'

Tony listened as Martin told him about the group and what they were up to. Strangely for him, he still felt relaxed. He enjoyed the casual chatter. Martin seemed like a nice guy and he ended up telling him a little about his work in Cyprus.

'Wow, sounds cool!' Martin exclaimed when he learned that Tony was a bodyguard.

'Not really,' laughed Tony, only half listening as Martin chatted on. His mind was elsewhere. I used to think my job was really cool, he thought sadly. These days I'm no more than a 'heavy', a debt collector and a bully. Tony knew Amin had turned him that way, and he'd let him. It was a long way from the ideals of the IKFF. He'd be in terrible trouble if they found out what he'd been up to. He also thought about his grandfather. He'd be so ashamed of his behaviour. Hurriedly Tony pushed the thoughts away, turning his attention back to Martin. The group had only been in town for a few days and Tony was able to tell him a bit about the area, places to visit and where to get the best food.

'Oh yeah, I've heard Michael Wright talk about some of those places,' Martin said, grateful for the tips. 'Actually you should come by and meet Michael. He's a great guy – from Northern Ireland, but he lives here now. He works for the church that brought us over here. I'm sure you'd get on really well with him.'

One of the girls came wandering over. 'Martin, we're ready. Are you coming?' she said, smiling warmly at Tony.

Martin stood to leave, then turned back. 'Hey, we haven't eaten yet. We'll probably get a take-out back at the apartments. Why don't you join us, Tony?'

Tony was a little taken aback. He didn't get such invitations very often. He'd normally be suspicious, but Martin had seemed very open and honest. He'd told him what the group was about. They were Christians and they wanted to tell everyone what they believed. They said it was good news and they genuinely seemed to want to help people. In the time they'd been talking together

Martin hadn't spouted any religious rubbish. Maybe Tony should go. He certainly didn't want to go home yet and the clubs had no appeal. Anyway, if it turns funny, I can easily handle myself, he thought.

'Yes, why not,' he said trying to smile.

✠   ✠   ✠

The rented apartment was like most of the other holiday lets in Limassol. It was quite tiny and there must have been fifteen young people all squashed together enjoying pizza. Martin introduced Tony and they made him very welcome, but he was relieved that they didn't ask too many questions or make a fuss over him.

There's something about them, thought Tony after a while as he looked around the happy room. But they could never imagine the sadness inside him. And what would they think if they knew what he was really like, some of the terrible things he'd done to people? They'd be terrified.

Again he heard mention of the name 'Michael Wright'.

'Oh, I wish Michael was here to meet you,' said one of the girls. She had sparkling eyes and a big smile. 'He loves talking to new people, especially anyone who lives in Cyprus. He loves this place.'

'Where is he?' Tony asked, hoping he sounded interested enough, although he really wasn't.

'Um, don't know tonight. Maybe just with his family. Or . . . no, actually he's probably up in Nicosia visiting the prison,' the girl said.

'Why not come to our church on Sunday,' interrupted Martin. 'You might meet him there.'

'Yeah, maybe,' said Tony doubtfully.

Tony stayed until it was getting late, and on the way home he thought about the group. He'd enjoyed the time in their company. They were good fun.

'Did I really say I might go to church?' he said to himself with a laugh. 'What was I thinking? They're just a bunch of weirdo Bible-bashers.' Still, something deep inside felt a little better. He hadn't felt so relaxed for a long time. Maybe he should seek them out again.

✠ ✠ ✠

Tony never made it to the church. A few days later he was walking along the street when a police car pulled up alongside him. Two Greek police officers got out, flashing their identity cards.

'Get in the car,' said one in broken English. Tony shook his head slowly, reaching inside his jacket for his diplomatic pass.

'Get in. Now!' the policeman said again, more sternly.

Tony swore rudely at him. 'You can't touch me,' he said, continuing to walk. Suddenly the second officer pulled out a pistol. Tony stopped and, looking at the gun, started laughing. He knew a lot about weapons.

'What are you going to do, shoot me with that ancient thing? I doubt it would fire!'

The policemen moved ahead of him, blocking his path. Tony smiled and lazily looked at his watch. It was his day off. He'd only been going for a haircut. He had nothing much to do.

'OK,' he said, smirking at them. 'If that's how you want to play it.' He decided to get in the car. They couldn't do anything to him, so he might as well play along. He'd go to the station, show his diplomatic pass and they'd let him go. At least he'd get a ride into town.

The station sergeant on duty didn't speak any English. He grinned like a fisherman who had just landed a prize catch as Tony was led into the dusty police station. He started speaking loud and fast in Greek. By now Tony understood a little of the language, but the words fell out of the sergeant's mouth in a torrent and there was no way he could keep up. Still, by the way the sergeant kept slapping a large black notebook, Tony gathered that he was being accused of a number of crimes. He remained calm. OK. Let them charge me, he thought. Then they'll release me on bail and I can sort it out from there. Even if they can pin something on me, I'll just get out of the country for a while, let the embassy sort it out.

Tony nonchalantly began reaching inside his jacket to pull out his diplomatic pass, but immediately the officers grabbed his arms, one on either side.

'Easy, easy,' he laughed at them. They obviously thought he was about to pull out a weapon. The sergeant barked something at the officers and they began to search him roughly.

At this, Tony grew more irritable. One of the men found his identity card and handed it to the sergeant.

'Ha!' he exclaimed in triumph as he put the pass in his own pocket.

'Just a minute,' said Tony. 'Give me that back. You haven't got a thing on me. Now give me the pass or I'll . . .' As Tony reached over the desk towards the sergeant, the other officers quickly slipped handcuffs on him.

Tony laughed, almost in disbelief. He could easily have got away from them. Indeed, he could have given them all a good seeing to and then gone about his business, but in a way he was enjoying the game. He even let himself be led to a cell down below the station. No point making a big fuss, he reasoned to himself. He didn't want Amin to hear of this. That would be embarrassing. No, instead he'd play along a little while longer.

'OK, OK,' he said, as the sergeant turned the giant key to the cell door, 'I won't make a scene, just get me someone from the British Embassy.' Tony knew that because of his identity card they'd have to contact an official. After that, it would only be an hour or so before he'd be released.

Tony was wrong. Hours went by. The cell was cold and damp. He hadn't eaten since breakfast and the guards had taken his cigarettes. Now he was getting angry. 'Hey, is anyone there?' he called out in English and then in Greek.

Silence.

No one could hear him. Or, rather, no one was listening. Tony slammed his fists at the iron bars. This wasn't what he'd expected. Where was the man from the embassy? He had studied international criminal law as part of his training. He knew they weren't allowed to hold him like this, at least not without allowing him a phone call or letting him see a lawyer.

'Hey you idiots,' he yelled at the top of his voice. 'Send someone down here immediately!' The now-familiar rage was starting to boil within him and he kicked at the bars until the whole cell echoed with the sound of clanging metal.

Still no response.

Where was everyone? What could he do? There was no one around and no way out. Tony was alone with the wild beast of his own rage.

20

TORTURED!

Tony awoke to the sound of men's voices. He had fallen asleep, slumped in the corner of the cell. He squinted through the bars at the clock on the far wall. It was 10 p.m. He jumped up, still angry at having been left. 'It's about time,' he muttered seeing the five Greek men. They weren't wearing uniforms, but Tony could tell they were police. Tony decided to keep a check on his temper and he squeezed his bitten nails into his palms. There was no point making things worse.

But instead of releasing him, the men handcuffed Tony again, securing his hands behind his back. They led him back upstairs to an interview room. That was OK, he'd expected to have to answer a few questions and sign some papers, but he could have done without the cuffs.

The officer in charge sat behind the desk and began lighting a cigarette. Sitting opposite, Tony looked at the large pile of files in front of him. Each one seemed to represent a local hotel. There were a couple of names he recognized; he'd stolen from them to get the money for his father. The others were unfamiliar.

'Mr Anthony, I am a reasonable man,' the officer began in heavily accented English. 'We know about all the robberies in these hotels and we have prepared this statement of confession for you. We just need you to sign here.'

The officer pushed a piece of paper and a pen towards Tony. It was all written in Greek. No way, Tony thought. I'm not signing anything I can't understand. By then he realized he was being accused of committing many crimes that he knew nothing about. Fair enough, he'd been caught. He'd admit to what he'd done, but he wasn't about to be locked up for anything else. He pointed to two of the files and nodded, but at the same time pushed the confession paper back towards the officer.

Immediately the officer grew angry. He wanted a full confession. Tony glared at him as the man rattled off a mixture of broken English and Greek, beads of sweat forming on the his brow. Tony shook his head. He knew the officer was trying to catch him out. It would be safer just to say nothing.

'I'm not saying anything until I can make a phone call,' Tony said, trying to sound reasonable. The officer scoffed and, muttering in Greek, he blew cigarette smoke into Tony's face. Now Tony was angry.

'I demand to speak to someone from the embassy.' It was as though the officer had been waiting for some display of defiance. Tony saw the whites of his eyes as suddenly the officer slapped his open palm across Tony's face.

'You demand nothing of me,' he spat.

Anger rose inside Tony. No one would treat him like this. He tasted blood from his split lip and it fed his rage. The cuffs bit into his wrists but he launched himself into a standing position and threw a high kick at the officer, sending him flying across the room. Immediately the other men were upon him, slapping, punching kicking. Tony fell to the floor, bracing himself against their continuing blows . . .

As day broke he found himself back in the dungeon cell, battered and bruised.

Another whole day passed by. Tony was given water, but nothing else. He saw no one. At precisely 10 p.m. the same group of men appeared. This time they shackled his arms and legs before taking him to the interrogation room. Tony refused to talk and received another severe beating.

The same thing happened the next night, and the next. Now there were more men, and they used truncheons and other weapons to beat and torture. They never wore uniforms so Tony knew this was not official police business. These were evil, corrupt men who seemed to be enjoying the 'sport' of beating their prisoner.

After five nights of torture Tony feared he could take no more. For much of his childhood his grandfather had beaten him, but this was different. Now he was weak from little food and utterly defenceless against these hard, brutal men.

I have to get out before I rot in here, Tony thought as the henchmen threw him back into the cell one night. He couldn't understand why nobody had come after him. Surely Amin would be missing him by now? Or perhaps no one even knew he was there!

By morning Tony had scraped his wrists so hard against the handcuffs that they were cut and bleeding badly. He lay on the floor, his head pounding, waiting for the morning officer to appear. It was always the same man. He wore a junior officer's uniform and brought water and dry bread. Tony had tried before to speak to him, wanting to tell him what was going on each night, but he would leave the food, making sure he didn't make eye contact. Each morning he scurried away like a frightened mouse. This morning Tony didn't even try to talk. He didn't even move. The officer came up close to the bars where he was slumped. He moaned in disgust when he saw Tony's bleeding arms and immediately looked scared. He spoke in Greek, trying to get Tony's attention, fearing he might be dead. Tony stirred.

'I told you, they are beating me,' he said weakly. 'Please, you've got to help me.' Tony looked pleadingly at him, hoping it would finally do the trick.

Within an hour two uniformed officers had taken Tony to the hospital. His plan was working. At the hospital the police removed the handcuffs for the doctor to treat his wounds. Thick bandages were placed around his wrists, making it impossible to put the handcuffs back on. Tony almost felt sorry for the officers as they led him back towards the waiting police car. He knew they would get into terrible trouble for allowing him to escape, but there was no way he was going back to the cells. In one quick kung fu move he did a speedy back flip to freedom. The officers were astonished. Tony started running, doing a zigzag pattern across the street whilst the officers fumbled to get their guns.

'Stop, stop, or I'll shoot,' he heard one of them cry.

They didn't fire and Tony ducked down the nearest alleyway running to freedom. He'd got away, but now he was on the run.

21

RUNNING SCARED

Before long the haunting wail of police sirens filled the air. This was a quiet area of Limassol and there were few people on the streets. Tony knew he could easily be spotted and picked up. He had to hide until dark. Most of all, he needed to find a safe place to sit and think – to work out what to do.

A little way ahead he noticed a narrow fire-escape ladder. Gritting his teeth against the agonizing pain in his wrists, he began climbing. The ladder rattled and creaked ominously, but Tony finally reached the top of the flat-roofed building. He squinted in the afternoon sunshine. It felt good on his face; he'd been in the dungeon for too long. From here he could see all across the town and he'd easily spot anyone on his tail. Already there were more police on the streets. They were looking for him. Taking no chances, he ducked down behind the perimeter wall. He knew he was in for a long wait.

Tony lay on his back, looking up at the clear blue sky. The same sky that hung over Canton, over the Shaolin temple and the Cold Mountain. Tony thought about the white tiger. Was she still roaming the slopes of Hanshan Si? How had her life changed? Did she have a mate, maybe some cubs even, or had she finally fallen foul of the hunter's snare? Tony realized that now he was like a hunted animal.

Lowsi had taught him not to fear anyone or anything. He'd taken him to the very edge of the scariest ridges of the highest mountains and made him perform t'ai chi blindfolded. He'd made him face the meanest street gangs in China, entered him in the toughest 'to the death' competitions and much, much more. And his training had worked; Tony feared nothing. He believed his martial arts and his own strength and supreme ability could get him out of anything. He felt the bandages on his arms and the bruises on his ribs. Pain didn't bother him much either. He was used to it. He'd grown up with his grandfather's cane. His body could endure almost anything.

So why was he shaking? Why did he feel so empty inside? Tony felt a strange hot, pricking sensation in his eyes. Before he knew it, a tear trickled down his cheek, followed by another one. Hurriedly Tony scrubbed at his face. He hadn't cried since those early days as a small child alone in China. He hadn't even cried when Aiya had been killed. His best friend had died, the only love he'd really known, but there had been no tears, just anger and bitterness. Sitting thinking about his life, Tony suddenly felt very, very empty, as if a deep black hole was opening up inside.

He didn't know what to do. He'd never allowed himself to feel alone, never felt vulnerable. What was he afraid of? He didn't know. All too soon Tony felt the familiar anger welling up inside. Still, at least it was better than tears and this frightening sense of emptiness. The anger was familiar and he could deal with it. If he hit out at someone or something he could control it, make it rest. *It's like a monster*, thought Tony. *It's eating me up inside. The more I feed it by lashing out, the more it wants.*

Tony put his head in his hands and tried to block it out. Digging deep within himself, he tried to find peace by meditation, the way Lowsi had taught him. But there was no peace there, just anger, and beneath, a sense of something new and yet dangerously familiar. It was something that had dwelt within him all his life, but he'd never allowed it to surface. It was desperate, agonizing loneliness.

Hours later, under cover of darkness, Tony made his way back to his apartment. He didn't know why, but he had an overwhelming need to speak to his parents. He didn't know what he was going to say, but he needed to get to them. If he could get out of Cyprus and get back to London, perhaps he'd be safe. Holding the phone close to his ear, he held his breath, waiting for the long-distance connection. At last he heard the familiar London tone.

'Come on, come on,' Tony whispered. 'Where are you? Come on, Mother, answer the phone.' He looked at the clock on the wall. It was early morning in the UK so they wouldn't be out.

'Come on, come on.' Perhaps they were still asleep in bed? But Tony knew his parents had always been early risers. Why weren't they answering the telephone? Finally Tony slammed down the receiver and slumped down on the floor with his head in his hands. He knew it wouldn't be long before the police caught up with him. He should have been planning his escape out of the country, but he seemed to have lost the plot. His mind was consumed with just one thing – speaking to his mother and father.

A couple of hours went by and still he couldn't reach them on the telephone. He made himself a sandwich, but didn't eat it. Finally he rang the woman who lived in the flat next door to his parents.

'Mrs Downing, this is Tony Anthony. I'm sorry to trouble you.'

There was a pause as the woman worked out who was speaking to her. 'Ah yes, Tony, in Cyprus. How are you?'

Tony ignored the question. 'I'm trying to reach my parents,' he said. 'It's a matter of urgency, but there's no reply from their phone.' There was another pause.

'Mrs Downing?' Tony prompted.

'But Tony, they are not here, they have gone.'

'Gone?' Tony was suddenly startled. 'What do you mean, gone?'

'They moved out a few days ago. We thought you must know. I still have the spare key. They've left a few things of yours in the flat, but otherwise it's empty. They've taken everything.'

'Where have they gone?' Tony asked, a sickening feeling growing in the pit of his stomach. Maybe they had gone to Switzerland for his father's treatment. But surely they'd have told him? And why would they move out of their London home?

'I'm sorry Tony, I –'

'Didn't they give you an address?' he interrupted, trying not to sound desperate.

'No, they didn't even say goodbye. We thought it was strange, but then they've always kept themselves to themselves haven't they? A van came, I think it was last Monday, then they were gone.'

Tony put the phone down, swallowing hard. Something nasty was starting to bubble inside. It wanted to burst out, up from his stomach and out of his mouth. The walls were closing in, and Tony could feel his heart pounding and his blood rushing through every vein, artery and capillary, trying to break out, break free.

'Get a grip,' he told himself. 'Pull yourself together.' Tony slammed his fist three times into the wall. He needed to feel something real, something painful, to stop the beast of his anger consuming him. He thought about the money he'd stolen for his parents. If it wasn't for them I wouldn't be in this situation, he reflected angrily. Yet deep inside he knew that wasn't the whole truth. The police wanted him in connection with the robberies, but Tony knew that he'd done far worse than that. If he ended up locked in prison for the rest of his life, he would deserve it. He knew that one day his past would catch up with him.

Over the next few hours Tony felt as though he was drowning in a sea of loneliness. His parents had abandoned him again. His one true love, Aiya, was gone. He hated life, hated himself, and hated what he had done to other people.

Tony found an old packet of cigarettes and began smoking them, one after another. The taste made him feel sick, but he drew heavily on the smoke, willing it to cloud out his rotten, stinking life.

Suddenly there was a loud knock at the door.

22

HELLHOLE

Tony wasn't thinking straight. Maybe he should have hidden himself. He hadn't put any lights on in the apartment. From the outside there was no sign he was in there. He might even have tried to escape. Or he could easily have gone out through the bedroom window and lowered himself, undetected, onto the street at the back of the building. But no, Tony got up off the floor, rubbing his head and eyes.

There was another insistent rap at the door. Without thinking, Tony went to the door and opened it.

'Stand still!' a voice barked.

Tony realized he was looking down the barrel of a gun. The policeman held it straight to his head. 'Don't even think of moving!'

Tony was trained to deal with this kind of situation. He noticed the tremor of the policeman's hand, holding the gun. He sensed the man was shocked and scared. He hadn't expected him to be there, hadn't imagined that he really would open the door. He wouldn't dare shoot. Yes, if he wanted, Tony could, even now, make his escape. But Tony was tired. He was tired of running, tired of fighting, tired of himself.

He recognized the policeman. He was the good one who had helped him get medical treatment the previous morning. Slowly Tony put both hands in the air.

'Don't worry,' he assured the officer. 'I won't do anything.'

'Why did you run?' the policeman asked, looking deep into
Tony's eyes and lowering his gun.

'I told you, they're beating me,' he said wearily.

'You know I have to take you back, don't you?' the policeman
said, holding out the handcuffs.

'You won't need those. I'll come with you, but please, you have
to do something to stop the beatings. And help me get in touch
with someone from the British Embassy,' Tony added, despair in
his voice.

'I'll see what I can do.'

In the police car Tony didn't bother plotting an escape. He
couldn't think of anything any more. He was tired and he didn't
care what happened.

That first night back Tony was beaten up again. He barely tried
to defend himself. With each kick and punch he thought of his
parents and the way they had abandoned him. He thought of his
grandfather's beatings and he thought of the young men who had
killed Aiya through their drunken stupidity. Tony had always
denied the robbery charges, but now he admitted to everything.
He gave no details, but just said 'yes', both to the crimes he had
committed and to many more that he hadn't. He just wanted to
be left alone.

The sergeant wiped his sweaty face and sat back in his chair
with a satisfied grin. He had Tony's signature and now he
could close the files. Triumphant, he shook with glee at his
victory.

'We're gonna put you away for a very long time, Mr Anthony,'
he said, standing up to give one last kick to Tony's beaten and
limp body.

✠   ✠   ✠

An ancient ceiling fan pushed stale air around the musty courtroom. Tony stood alone and silent. Since his confession, a man from the British Embassy had been to see him and arranged for a lawyer to represent him in court. The man's superior manner had irritated Tony.

'It's not looking good,' he'd warned Tony. 'Don't expect any preferential treatment just because you've got a British passport. In fact, depending on which judge you get, that could be a disadvantage.'

'Can't you do anything for me? Tony had asked, tired and frustrated.

'I'm afraid you signed the confession . . .'

'Yeah, under torture,' Tony interrupted.

'It's a sensitive time politically right now. Your diplomatic status doesn't count for much.' The man had seemed resigned to Tony's fate. There was nothing he could do. Tony sensed he was being abandoned to the mercy of a Cypriot court.

Tony struggled to understand what was being said. In a series of quick-fire conversations the two lawyers argued between themselves in Greek. Nobody translated. Meanwhile the judge just looked bored and disdainful. Eventually he looked at his watch and raised a large, fleshy hand to silence the court. He had heard enough. It was time to pass sentence.

'Three years in prison.' Tony sat with his head bowed. He was too sick and tired to bother caring. An hour later he was on his way to Nicosia Central Prison. It was Christmas Eve.

✠   ✠   ✠

Tony stood in silence as two prison officers went through the registration process. They took his photograph and fingerprints, all the time chatting to each other, cigarettes dangling idly from their mouths. It was as though Tony didn't really exist. This was something they did every day. They didn't care who he was, what he had done, or what he was about to face.

Finally one of them pushed a rough and ragged blanket at Tony, along with a bar of soap, toilet paper and a shaving razor. A stale odour lingered on the blanket. Tony wondered how many men it had belonged to and whether it had ever been washed. One of the officers signalled for Tony to follow the other one. He could feel the anger beginning to rise inside. They couldn't even do him the courtesy of speaking directly to him. Still, he had a feeling that far worse was yet to come. He dug his torn fingernails into his palms, trying to control the beast within.

The prison was a large, forbidding place, with crumbling stone walls and shafts of light breaking in at random from the low ceiling. Here and there water dripped down ancient channels, making the whole place smell of damp and decay. Now they were heading down. There was less natural light, and a single electric bulb cast an eerie hue on the walls of the tunnel leading into the depths of the prison. As they reached a set of narrow, steep steps the stench rose up, filling Tony's lungs with a sickening smell of rot. He gulped. Panic was beginning to take hold.

The stairs opened out into a long corridor of cells. Tony squinted in the low, artificial light, noting the heavy iron door at the end. Screaming, yelling and hysterical laughter echoed off the stone walls and metal bars. He concentrated on his breathing. Long, deep breaths. Stay calm. Don't lose control.

Soon the guards stopped and began unlocking the door to one of the larger cells. They gestured towards a lower bunk and pushed Tony forward.

He took in the details of the cell, his heart pounding loud and heavy. It was as though he had been led into hell itself. Tony clamped a hand over his mouth and nose. It reeked of urine and sweat. His eyes fell on the seven iron bunk beds that were secured to the floor by heavy chains. His stomach leaped, sending bile into his mouth. Men lay like living corpses on each bed. Some cowered into the walls, hugging their ribs while gently rocking, grunting or humming. Others were, in some way, abusing themselves or each other.

'No!' he heard himself scream. 'No, no way!'

With an iron fist he hit out, sending one of the officers crashing to the ground. Madness and panic took hold. He had to get out, had to smash his way through the horror and decay. There was no way he could stay here; no way he could be part of this nightmare. He lashed out at everyone and everything, causing uproar. Slop buckets went flying as men leaped up from their beds. Some joined in the chaos, hitting out at Tony and each other. Others screamed, adding to the frenzy as they tried to avoid flaying fists and kicks. Like a wild animal Tony tried to smash his way through the cell, until suddenly a blow to the back of his head knocked him to the floor.

For a moment Tony couldn't catch his breath. He felt his head hit the stone floor, and then everything seemed to be swimming. He tried to get up, but truncheon blows rained down on him. Guards appeared from nowhere and roughly wrestled his arms behind his back, securing them with a thick leather belt.

The next thing he knew, Tony was out in the sunlight, being half-dragged, half-carried across cobblestones. He gulped to drink in the fresh air. Every inch of his body throbbed with pain and he soon slipped back into unconsciousness.

23

CAGED TIGER

Tony awoke in almost darkness, his body burning with pain. It was freezing cold. What was that? An eerie scratching and rustling noise close by. He blinked hard, trying to make sense of his surroundings. A single candle fought to cast its dim light into the blackness. It flickered dangerously in the howling draught coming under the iron door. Tony focused every sense he had on the flame, as though to look away might snuff out its life forever.

In those first waking moments panic gripped him. Not taking his eyes off the light, he frantically ran his hands over the cold stone walls. He felt grit and thick dust on what seemed to be a small wooden bench he was lying on. There were shadows moving across the floor. No. They weren't shadows. Now he knew the source of the scurrying, scratching noises. Cockroaches. Hundreds of them!

Tony hugged his knees to his chest, making himself as small as possible. As he moved, pain shot through his body. Tentatively he pressed his skin and limbs, feeling his wounds. There didn't seem to be anything too serious, no obvious broken bones, just heavy bruising, and his head was pounding from the truncheon blow. He shivered. The cell was icy cold, but sweat was dripping off him as though he were in a sauna.

Fear gripped him. It wasn't something he was used to. Suddenly he was like a caged tiger, terrified and desperate to get out. He tried to stand, but the ceiling of the cell was so low that he banged his head, sending pain careering through his body.

'Get a grip, keep hold of yourself,' he said through gritted teeth. 'Stay in control.' In his mind's eye Tony saw his grandfather's face. He knew what he must do. Meditate. Harness the inner peace, the chi. He breathed deeply and closed his eyes, but the blackness just closed in on him. There was no peace, just a vile black hole of terror.

✢   ✢   ✢

Tony lost track of how long he was kept in solitary confinement – the 'hole' – they called it. Night and day were the same in there. But at last he was moved back to the main cells.

'Ah, so you survived the hole then.'

A young man stood in the open doorway of Tony's new cell. The prison authorities had decided it was safer to give him a cell to himself. That way he wouldn't smash anyone up. It was only just wide enough for Tony to be able to stretch out both arms without hitting the walls. There was a hard bed, with a thin and worn mattress, and a tin slop bucket in the corner. Tony hadn't expected a visitor. He said nothing.

'They say it either drives you totally crazy or it breaks you,' the stranger continued. 'Mind you, it makes no difference in this place, if you ask me. Might as well be mad.'

'That so?' said Tony, not showing much interest in the unexpected guest.

'I'm Andy,' the man said, stepping into the cell and offering his hand. 'From Yorkshire, travelling with the army. Got two years

for fraud. Silly git,' he laughed. Tony hesitated and then took his
hand.

'Tony,' he said solemnly.

'I know, there's been a lot of talk about you. We heard you
nearly smashed your way out of your first cell. Caused some
serious damage, eh?' Tony said nothing. 'Good thing, fighting
skills, round here. It's every man for himself. You'll soon work
that out.'

Andy was around Tony's age. He looked fit and much cleaner
than a lot of the other prisoners.

'It's good to have another English guy around,' he said, sitting
down on Tony's bed. 'It's mainly Greeks, Arabs and Turks in here.
There are a few Palestinians and a couple of Israelis. They keep
them on different wings, of course, in case they try to kill each
other. You'll get used to the politics in here. There's always some
kind of feud.'

Tony shook his head slowly. He wasn't interested. He just wanted
to keep himself to himself. Then again, he had to admit, it was nice
to see a friendly face and Andy's chatter brought a flicker of warmth
into the icy cell.

'Don't worry, mate,' said Andy, sensing Tony's sadness. 'The
first few weeks are always the worst. Then you sort of get used to
it. A man like you can take care of yourself anyway.'

Tony snorted a cynical laugh in reply.

'They're not a bad lot really,' Andy said, nodding towards the
other cells. Then he laughed, 'Well, not considering they're all
thieves, murderers, fraudsters, terrorists . . . They're just like you
and me really.'

Tony looked at him doubtfully.

'It's just the mad ones you have to watch out for,' Andy
continued, making Tony smile a little.

'No, mate, I mean it. I suppose back home they'd be banged up in some mental institution. The "criminally insane" they'd call them. Here, they're just thrown in with the rest of us. There's some serious nutters, I tell you, they'll cut you up just for entertainment. Look . . .' Andy pulled up his shirtsleeve, revealing sore-looking burns. He ran his fingers over the wounds. 'This was just last week. Alcaponey, we call him, first-class nutcase. Big geezer, built like a giant. Ugly too, you'll soon spot him. He cornered me and did this with his cigarette. Laughing all the time, he was. There was nothing I could do. Mind you, he could have done a lot worse than this. You'll hear the stories . . .'

Andy's voice tailed off and his mind seemed to wander – to a dark and terrifying place.

'Thanks for the warning, mate,' said Tony, trying a little harder now to be friendly. He was beginning to realize that it might not be a bad thing to have a few friends after all. Here, at least, was someone to pass the time with, and Andy seemed like a good bloke.

'So tell me, when do you get to take a shower in this place?'

Andy looked at him warily. 'Well, you can go to the washroom anytime you want, but never go alone, is what I'd say. It's a dangerous place. A lot of the madmen hang out there.'

'What about the guards?' Tony asked.

'They only go near to drag out someone who's been beaten up. Anyway, they turn a blind eye to what goes on. Some of them are as twisted as the madmen anyway,' Andy spat bitterly. 'Me and some of the other lads will go down later on, so I'll give you a shout. Don't expect luxury though and don't expect hot water. Sometimes there's no water at all and it comes out of ancient rusty pipes. You might think some of us have suntans, but it's just the brown stuff we wash in.' He laughed.

Tony wasn't surprised. He'd heard that Nicosia Central Prison was one of the worst prisons in the world. It was a pit, a hellhole, where the men were left to rot, and many did. Many of the guards were corrupt and they didn't care about the fights and injustices between the prisoners. If someone got badly beaten, they just came and cleared up the mess, carting them off to the infirmary or, in some cases, straight to the mortuary.

Tony quickly discovered there was little organization, except that prisoners were given three meals a day and on most days they could walk out into the courtyard for twenty minutes' exercise. He looked forward to these times. There was nothing to see, just more stone and cement, but at least there was blue sky and the atmosphere was fresher. Although the weather was bitter, it felt warmer outside than within the stone walls of the prison block. The cold was the prison's natural torture system. Day after day, Tony woke up shivering, breathing cloudy vapour into the pungent air. The prisoners wore only flip-flops and their feet were permanently numb with cold. They burned anything they could get their hands on, making small fires to crowd around in the evenings. A fire was a small but priceless pleasure. Somehow though, it made things harder when the men were locked in their cells, struggling through the night alone in the biting cold. Tony always slept with his arms wrapped around his head and ears, trying to shut out the weeping and hysterical screaming that came from many other cells. Even the toughest men could be heard crying like babies on some freezing nights.

During the day they could roam around as they pleased, but there was very little to do. They lived in filth and squalor. No wonder many of them turned into little more than living corpses. Many took drugs and everyone chained-smoked. It was easy to understand why. Sometimes they were served cold, lumpy porridge made with water for breakfast. Otherwise, every meal was the same. It was disgusting, but Tony was determined to eat to keep his strength up.

'They wouldn't serve this to pigs back home,' he mused with Andy and a couple of others as they all picked the mould off the hard lumps of bread.

'I see tomatoes are in season again,' said Shane, a young Sri Lankan. The others laughed. They were given rotten tomatoes with every meal.

'You know, if I close my eyes, I can imagine these blackened eggs are actually beautifully scrambled with butter and a touch of cream,' said Mohammed. The others sniggered.

'Yeah, I can taste the smoked salmon, too,' said Andy. 'And, hey, gentlemen, a champagne toast . . . to better days'

The men laughed.

'To better days,' they said in unison, raising their tin cups before downing the disgusting black liquid that was supposed to be coffee.

'Here we go lads, keep quiet then.' It was Stavros, a Greek who liked to hang around with the English speakers. He was serving a life sentence. No one knew exactly what for. He'd already been in prison for ten years. He scurried around the place like a ferret and was a useful man to know. Stavros had links with 'the outside' and could get hold of things. Tony suspected he was a main supplier of drugs, but he could also sometimes get paper, pens, books and magazines.

'What have you got?' whispered Andy eagerly as the group crowded in, heads low.

'Steak,' he whispered back, his eyes twinkling with excitement. Checking that no one outside the group was watching, he dug into the waistband of his trousers and pulled out a ragged-looking cloth parcel.

'Whoa!' exclaimed Andy.

Shane whistled through his teeth in admiration. 'Don't know how you do it,' he said as Stavros began to peel away pieces of cloth.

'I got this thing going with the cook,' he winked. 'Cost me a week's worth of fags, mind.'

Instantly the other men dug into their pockets and handed Stavros a couple of cigarettes each. He grinned in delight.

'Now, here she is, what a beauty!' With trembling fingers he pulled back the last piece of cloth to reveal a small, shrivelled piece of cooked meat. Hungrily he tore it into equal pieces. There was barely a mouthful between the five men.

Tony put the meat in his mouth, chewing and sucking, being careful not to swallow too soon. The meat was leathery and tasted of nothing much other than salt. Still, treats like this were few and far between. The men sat in silence, twisting their tongues and grinding the 'feast' between their teeth, savouring every morsel.

✝   ✝   ✝

The weeks passed by painfully slowly and winter turned to summer. If the winter chill was hard, the heat of the Cypriot summer was even more gruelling. The prison block was like a furnace and tempers ran higher than ever. There were more fights and it wasn't unheard of for a prisoner to be beaten and killed over a cigarette.

Tony had no contact with the outside world. There's nobody to care anyway, he thought bitterly, as each day he watched the other prisoners poring over letters from their loved ones. He'd never heard from his parents and still didn't know why they'd disappeared. He hadn't been in touch with Lowsi since he'd started doing debt collection work for Amin. Tony cringed when he thought of how this work had dishonoured his grandfather and the way of kung fu.

Whenever he could get hold of paper and paint Tony spent hours doing artwork. It took him back to the house in Canton where he had painted and practised Chinese writing as a young boy. But there were few other happy memories of that time. His grandfather's home had been as much a prison as this place, Tony reflected angrily. Closing his eyes, he could clearly remember the torture of some of his early training. Thwack! Tony winced, almost feeling the strike of his grandfather's bamboo cane beating him around his ears.

Tony scrubbed his paintbrush against the paper, making angry lines of thick black paint. All his life he had been like a caged animal. He had never been free. Only his beloved Aiya had really cared for him, she was the only person to have come close to touching that deep black hole of loneliness inside him. Why did she have to die? It wasn't fair! Tony ripped up the paper he was working on, screwing it up into a ball and violently slamming it to the floor.

'Hey, what's up with you today?'

It was Andy. Tony wasn't in the mood for chat.

'The old place getting to you, eh? Well we all have days like that in here.'

Tony sat still, his eyes fixed on the floor, his bitten fingernails pressed into his palms as he battled to control the anger inside him. He didn't want to lash out at Andy. He meant him no harm. He didn't deserve a beating.

'Look mate, I know what it's like. Sometimes you just need someone to talk to,' Andy said, seating himself down next to Tony.

Tony snorted and didn't look up.

'There's this guy whose been visiting me. His name's Michael Wright . . .'

Suddenly Tony was listening. Michael Wright. Michael Wright. The name rang around in his head.

'I know that name,' he said, turning to look at Andy. 'Why do I know that name?'

'Dunno mate. He's some preacher man from Belfast – a missionary, he calls himself. Lives on Cyprus, he does. Bit of a do-gooder, y'know, but he comes to visit me every week . . .'

Of course. Tony remembered the evening just before the police caught up with him when he'd met the young British student in that square in Limassol. He'd gone back to Martin's apartment and met others who were working at the church. They'd all talked about Michael Wright. Yes . . . Michael Wright, the missionary from Ireland. It had to be the same man.

'So?' said Tony, pleased that he'd worked out the connection, but now no longer interested.

'Well, I hope you don't mind, but I was talking to him about you.' Tony said nothing.

'He'd really like to meet you,' offered Andy tentatively.

'And what would I need with a preacher?' snapped Tony.

'OK, OK. Just thought I'd mention it,' Andy said, a little nervously. 'Look man, it's up to you – but you're like me. You don't get any visitors and sometimes this place can really get to you. Seeing Michael won't do you any harm. You just let him witter on about stuff and at least you get a coke out of it.'

Suddenly Tony was interested again. 'Coca-Cola, you mean?'

'Yeah,' laughed Andy, relaxing. 'There's a canteen in the visitors' room. If you have a visitor they're allowed to buy you a can.'

Tony could almost feel the cool refreshing liquid on his tongue.

It had been so long. It was awfully tempting. He wiped a dirty hand across his sweaty brow. Many a man in his situation would do anything for a taste of the outside, but Tony had too much pride. He didn't need a preacher. He didn't need anyone. And why would this preacher man be interested in him? He shook his head, stood up and walked off towards his cell, anger once again burning inside.

24

THE LETTER

A few days later Tony woke to see a white envelope being pushed under his door. He stared at it for a second. He had now been in prison for four months and had never received any mail. His heart leaped. Could it be from his parents? He flung himself off his bed and grabbed the envelope, wiping it clean of dust and grit. His heart sank. It wasn't his mother's handwriting and it had a Cypriot stamp. It had been posted locally. Still, curiosity got the better of him and he ripped open the envelope, eager to see who it was from. He read down the page quickly. The signature at the bottom was 'Michael Wright'. Tony drew in a deep breath, and then read it again and again, poring over each word as though it were a precious lifeline.

Tony didn't know quite what to think about the letter. There was still so much anger inside him. Why was this preacher writing to him? What did he want from him? Why would he want to interfere in his life? The answers were all there on the page. Michael's letter was friendly. He explained that he and his wife had come over from Belfast and were working with a church in Limassol. They had heard about Tony from the local newspapers and were worried about him. 'We know you are a long way from home,' the letter said, 'and I hope I can come and visit you.'

'Why?' asked Tony. 'Why would a man like you want to visit someone like me?'

'I simply want to visit you because of the love of Jesus,' he read.

Tony felt a strange giddiness rising inside him. An urge to laugh broke through his anger and irritation. What a strange thing to say, he thought. Yet he read the phrase over and over again, as if in disbelief.

Tony read on, learning a little more about Michael Wright, until he came to his signature at the bottom of the letter. Next to it Michael had drawn a small smiley. Tony shook his head in disbelief, feeling the anger beginning to take hold again. A smiley face? How dare this man, this stranger, draw a happy, smiling face?

'I am *in prison*,' said Tony out loud and through gritted teeth. 'What have I got to smile about?' He screwed up the letter and threw it into the corner of the room. Angrily he began pacing up and down like a caged tiger, the words of the letter ringing in his ears.

Tony was irritated and angry all day. It was gruellingly hot and when a fight broke out between some Arabs and Israelis, Tony was quick to join in. He didn't care what the fight was about. He just wanted the action. It gave him a way to vent his anger. He didn't care who he punched or kicked. Adrenaline shot through his veins and he lashed out in a frenzy, smashing and breaking anything and anyone in his path. But the fight quickly got out of hand. Soon almost every prisoner was involved and all manner of weapons appeared from nowhere. There were knives, truncheons, blades and batons. The guards fired gunshots in the air, trying to get the prisoners under control, but they were ignored. The men had so little to lose. Many didn't care if they got shot. At least the fight gave them something to do, something to beat the dreadful boredom.

Finally the guards called for reinforcements. The army arrived, blazing their machine guns, barking orders over loudspeakers. Eventually everyone was rounded up and locked in their cells.

Sitting on his bed later, Tony nursed a sore fist and played back scenes from the battle in his head. It had felt good to lash out again, but now he was coming down from the rush of excitement. He pictured the faces he'd smashed up and winced, disgusted at himself.

From the corner of his eye, Tony caught sight of Michael's letter, still lying crumpled up in the corner. He stared at it for a while, then went over and picked it up. Straightening it out he read it again, and then a second and third time. He'd read it so many times now that he could almost memorize the words.

What harm could a preacher do? Maybe Andy was right. Maybe he needed to see someone from the outside world. Tony dusted the grit off the paper. He was sick of the dirt, sick of the squalor. Perhaps half an hour out of this pit might be good. The thought of that Coca-Cola was very, very tempting. He'd also heard you could get chocolate. What he wouldn't do for a Mars bar! Maybe he would agree to let this Michael Wright visit him. After all, he thought, if he does anything dodgy, I can easily smash his face in.

Tony rubbed his aching fist with his other hand and lay down to sleep.

25

THE STRANGER VISITS

The following Thursday, Tony was led up to the visitors' room. It had the same musty smell of decay as the rest of the prison, but the air was certainly fresher. Sunshine streamed in through the windows, its rays dancing mischievously on the badly white-washed walls as they picked up a reflection from a guard's watch or set of keys. A ceiling fan, though cranky and old, pushed a welcome breeze through the stifling heat. To a visitor this was an intimidating, hideous place, but to a prisoner just up from the pit beneath, it was close to heavenly.

Tony instantly spotted the small canteen in the corner. His throat ached permanently these days from the dust and heat. He chewed on his dry tongue and looked around at the other prisoners and their visitors.

The prisoners sat on one side of a long, narrow, wooden table with their guests seated opposite. Many of the men held hands across the table with their wives, girlfriends, mothers and children. The room was noisy with chatter. Some of the women were crying and the children were restless with the heat.

Tony stared into the space opposite him. So where was Michael? Tony was surprised to feel nervous at the thought of a visitor. It had been a long time since he'd talked to anyone from the outside. He was suddenly aware of what he must look like. It was difficult to shave properly with the blunt blades they were given and he knew he badly needed a haircut. He felt foolish. What was he doing, meeting a complete stranger like this? What would he say to him? What did Michael expect of him? Tony chewed nervously at the skin around his ragged fingernails. He looked again at the drinks machine. No, this was foolish. He felt stupid waiting and was just about to signal to one of the guards that he wished to leave, when the door opened.

A tall, bearded man was shown into the room. The guard escorted him towards Tony and instructed him to sit down opposite. He wore a beaming smile, nylon slacks and a crumpled patterned shirt, with sleeves slightly too short. What an idiot! thought Tony. He looks like Father Christmas on holiday.

'Tony, it's so good to meet you. I've heard so much about you,' said Michael in a Northern Irish accent as he thrust out a large suntanned hand. 'Thank you for allowing me to come and visit.'

Tony was wary. What had he heard? What did this man think he knew about him? He offered his hand without meeting Michael's eyes. Michael instantly grabbed Tony's hand in both of his and shook it warmly. Tony didn't like that. He didn't want to be rude, but he was very suspicious of Michael. He had been raised to trust no one. In the past year anger had fed that distrust, and prison life was making him even more paranoid and suspicious of everyone. Why should Michael be this friendly? Why should he travel all the way from Limassol to Nicosia, a two-hour round trip, just to see him.

Michael recognized Tony's anguish. 'Tony, I'm here to be a friend to you,' he said, still smiling, but speaking in a gentle, almost hushed voice. 'You know who I am. But Tony, I'm not here to preach to you. I just want to be a mate . . .'

Tony looked up scornfully. Yeah, sure! he thought, but said nothing.

'I just want you to know that there are people outside who really care for you,' Michael continued. 'Everyone at our church is praying for you and we want to support you as much as we can.'

Suddenly there was weeping and wailing. A young Greek prisoner was saying goodbye to his parents. Both mother and father were crying and the guards had to break the family embrace, firmly leading the prisoner away. Tony thought of his own parents. They would never visit him somewhere like this. He doubted they even knew he was here. They didn't care enough to find out where he was. They'd taken the money he'd stolen for them and abandoned him. Fury started to rise within.

He glanced up at Michael. Just who was this guy? Tony was fighting a battle in his head. He wanted to let his anger out at someone. It would have been easy to grab Michael and to teach the preacher a good lesson for interfering in his life. Instead, Tony drew in a deep breath, trying to calm himself. It wasn't fair to lash out at Michael. After all, he was a complete stranger, yet he'd taken the trouble to visit. Tony couldn't understand why, but he did genuinely seem to care.

While the battle raged in Tony's head Michael had started to talk. Tony didn't pay much attention at first. He was struggling with his own anger and confusion. But soon he'd tuned in to Michael's chatter. He didn't care to say much back, but he began to listen as the preacher told him a little about his life and his family. Before long a harsh bell sounded; visiting time was over. Michael stood up slowly, once again beaming all over his face.

'Thank you again for letting me visit you, Tony,' he said, once again offering his hand. 'If it is OK with you, I would like to come back again. Maybe next Thursday?'

Tony didn't know what to say, but he gave a slight nod, still not meeting Michael's gaze.

'God bless you, Tony. I will look forward to seeing you again soon.' With that, Michael was gone.

Idiot, thought Tony, cursing him under his breath. He watched as the preacher was led through the security gates. Just what was he up to? Tony shook his head, as if in disbelief that the strange encounter had actually taken place. He drained the very last drop of Coca-Cola, savouring the sweet, cool sensation it left in his mouth. Perhaps the visit had been worthwhile after all.

As the guards led him back down to the dungeon Tony realized he was smiling. He didn't know why. Maybe it was the Coca-Cola. Still, as the familiar stench of the grave-like cells rose to greet him, revulsion and hatred wrapped around him like a cloak. He pictured Michael's smiling face and imagined him driving home in the sunshine to his perfect life. He felt as though the prison walls were laughing at him as they dragged him down, deeper and deeper into the pit of despair. He spat at the floor and slapped the cackling wall in anger.

26

A LIFELINE

The next week Michael was early. His face beamed as Tony rose from the darkness into the light of the visitors' room. Michael was already enjoying a Coca-Cola and he pushed another ice-cold can towards Tony as he sat down. Tony took the drink gratefully, taking deep slurps of the nectar-like liquid as Michael began his chatter.

'Ah, doesn't it taste good in this heat?' Michael exclaimed, rolling his sleeves back and wiping his brow. 'D'you know, I've been in Cyprus for three years now, but I still can't get used to it.'

Tony couldn't help but smile. 'You should feel the heat down there,' he said, gesturing towards the door he'd just come through.

Michael chatted about the things he liked and the things he didn't like about Cyprus. As the visit drew to a close Tony realized he had enjoyed listening, though he was barely prepared to admit it to himself. Most of the time he stared straight down at the table, but as Michael talked Tony found himself picturing the scenes in his head. Michael was a window to the outside world. Tony could imagine some of the people Michael described who went to his church. He could picture the teenagers having a great time on their youth camp in the Troodos Mountains. He could remember the taste of good Turkish coffee through hearing about Michael's visits to the *kafeneions*. Michael couldn't speak much Greek, and Tony smiled to think of him trying to strike up conversations with the old Greek men who could always be found in those traditional coffee bars in the mornings.

Just before Michael left, he asked if he could pray for Tony. Tony didn't know what to say, so he just nodded. Tony didn't understand this idea of praying. He'd seen pictures in books of children, kneeling by their bedsides, their eyes closed and their hands clasped together. He also remembered Mr Sizer, his RE teacher at school, talking about a prayer that Jesus taught in one of the Bible stories. That had all been a long time ago, but here was Michael Wright, sitting right in front of him, eyes closed, talking as though God was listening to him, as though God was right there in the room with them.

What an idiot, thought Tony. He's talking into thin air.

' . . . Lord Jesus, please take care of my friend, Tony. Thank you that you love him. Please give him patience and peace in the difficult days . . . Amen,' finished Michael.

Tony fidgeted uncomfortably, looking around to see if anyone was watching and wishing Michael would be quick to leave.

After that, Michael came back to see Tony every Thursday, week after week. Between visits Michael wrote and often sent him books. Tony was grateful. Reading helped fight the boredom. It would be easy to go crazy in prison, there was so little to do, day after day. Tony battled to keep his mind sharp, learning languages from the other inmates, and Michael's parcels of books were a lifeline. He had to guard them well though. The pages made rich pickings for prisoners to use as roll-ups for cigarettes, toilet paper or fire starters.

As time went on Tony realized how much he looked forward to seeing Michael each week. He still thought it strange, but now when Michael prayed, Tony tried to imagine that God, whoever he might be, really was listening.

If for some reason Michael couldn't make a visit, he made sure someone else from his church came instead. Tony had been astounded one day to see a little, grey-haired lady waiting for him.

'I'm Valerie,' she said, holding out a wrinkled hand.

What must she think, coming to a place like this and visiting a person like me? thought Tony, ashamed. But Valerie had the same confident smile as Michael.

'You know, the Lord Jesus has blessed me so much through my life, young man,' Valerie told him. 'I just want to share his goodness. It must be terrible for you in here, but I want you to know that I pray for you every day and there are many people in our church who care for you.'

Six months ago this kind of talk would have caused Tony's blood to boil. He'd have been angry and suspicious, worried about who these people were and what they wanted from him. But Valerie was so gentle, so loving. She looked at Tony in the same way as he'd noticed many of the Greek mothers looking at their sons in prison. There were tears in her eyes as she said goodbye to him, and yet that beautiful smile never left her face.

Tony had never told anyone about his crimes. Although his name had been all over the newspapers, no one knew what he was really like. Could people like Valerie or Michael ever cope with knowing the depths of his evil crimes? Robbery was one thing, but the way he'd left people beaten, broken, and maimed for life was quite another. And this God, this Jesus, they talked about, if he was real, he would know everything. Tony could never be like the people at church. They were good people. God would never want anything to do with a man like him.

Tony hated himself. He hated what he'd done, who he had become. There were days when he thought he might go crazy, locked away in the prison, but he still believed he deserved to be there. He would never argue with that. Most of the other prisoners moaned about their sentences, but Tony believed that if he had to spend the rest of his life in prison, he would be getting what he deserved. What was there to come out to anyway? His family had never been interested in him. Aiya was gone. Even his kung fu was not what it once was. Sometimes when he had been working long hours as a bodyguard, he had stayed up all night to make sure he completed his t'ai chi routines and meditation. Now he had all the time in the world, but he rarely worked on his moves and he didn't have the patience or peace of mind for meditation.

The quest in meditation had always been to find 'enlightenment'. That might have been possible when life was going well for Tony, but with his life being tested in this dungeon, the religion of his grandfather did nothing for him. These days he wasn't sure what he believed any more. If enlightenment did exist, he was a long way from reaching it.

Every time he closed his eyes Tony was haunted by painful scenes from his past. Most days he woke up angry. He'd lie on his bunk, smoking cigarettes until the door was unlocked and he could join the others for the breakfast slop.

Today was no different. In fact, today Tony felt even more angry than usual. He was thinking about Michael Wright. The preacher would be coming to see him again this afternoon. Earlier in the week he'd sent Tony a Bible. Tony had tried reading some of it, but he'd soon got frustrated and now it was lying in the corner next to the slop bucket. Tony had thrown it there in a temper the night before.

Michael's trying to brainwash me, Tony thought, viciously stubbing his second cigarette butt against the wall and lighting up another. Yes, that's it. He wants me to join some strange cult or something. I've heard of things like this before. Tony played around with the idea in his head, growing more and more angry. Why else would he be so nice to me? he reasoned. Maybe he thinks I've got some money stashed away that I might give to his stupid church, he thought, now beginning to pace the room.

'Come on, come on,' he shouted out loud. These days he rarely felt hungry, but the nights were so long and he hated feeling like a caged animal, locked in his cell. Surely it was breakfast time? He could smell it.

'Come on, where are you?' he yelled at the guards, now banging on the door. A guard shouted back, swearing and telling him to shut up. Tony recognized the voice. It was one of the guards everyone most hated. He was sick. He enjoyed seeing the prisoners suffering. It was well known that if he was on duty, any fights could break out. He'd always turn a blind eye while blood was being shed.

Tony swore back at him in Greek, knowing that now he would be last to be let out.

Back and forth he paced, still thinking about Michael Wright. He could see his smile. He's laughing at me, Tony thought. Yes, that's it. He's as sick as the guard outside. He just likes to see people suffering. Well, I'll teach him a lesson. This afternoon I'll give him one chance to tell me the truth, to tell me why he is visiting me like this. If he can't give me a good answer, I'll grab him and punch his face.

At last the key turned in the lock. Tony sprang to the door, fighting an urge to throw his fist into the guard's face.

Tony sat alone for breakfast, drinking the cold weak coffee, but leaving the bowl of lumpy porridge untouched. He didn't want to

talk to anyone today. He would keep himself to himself until
visiting time. Then he would confront Michael.

27

THE TRUTH

By the afternoon Tony's blood was boiling. Fury surged through his veins. All day he had brooded over his so-called friend. No, Michael Wright was no friend. He was up to something, Tony was sure. Today Tony was going to confront him, to find out what all this was about, once and for all.

The visiting room was crowded with Greek families. Usually they distracted Tony, but today he was focused only on one thing. Drumming his fingers on the table in front of him, he pictured Michael's grinning face, plotting what he would do to him. It would be easy to grab him by the beard and yank him over the table. OK, so he'd be locked in the hole, but he'd have taught Michael a lesson, that's for sure. It would be worth it.

Where was he? Why was Michael keeping him waiting? 'He's playing with me, even now.' Tony whispered to himself, his teeth clenched, blood running hot and wild in his veins.

The door opened and in walked Michael, looking hot and dishevelled.

'Tony, I'm so sorry,' he began, 'the traffic in Nicosia was terrible today . . .'

Michael stopped mid-sentence, immediately sensing Tony's anger.

'Tony, what's wrong?' he asked, concerned, pulling up his chair close to the table and leaning forward.

Tony said nothing and refused to look into Michael's face. That's right, he thought, the monster of his anger raging within. Come closer, I can easily grab you now.

'Tony? What is it?'

'Why do you keep coming here, Michael?' finally Tony spoke, aggression seething out of him.

'You know why, Tony,' he said calmly, sitting back in his chair. 'I visit you because of Jesus, because God wants me to tell you about him.' He paused.

Should I just grab him now? Tony wondered.

Just get on with it, urged the monster within.

No, not yet, he reasoned. Give him a chance.

'God loves you Tony,' said Michael.

Tony swore. 'OK. So if this God of yours really exists, why doesn't he just show up and do something?'

'He has. He is doing something, even now. What do you think I've been doing all these months, Tony? What about Valerie and the other people who have visited you?'

'Yeah, what about them?'

'They have been showing you God. Showing you his love, showing you that he cares for you.'

'Right, so is this God chicken or something,' Tony scoffed sarcastically. 'Can't he show up himself? Why should I believe he exists when I can't even see him?'

'Do you believe in gravity Tony? Do you believe in air, or wind, or love?'

Tony hesitated, wondering where this was heading.

'You do, don't you?' Michael continued. 'Just because you can't see these things doesn't mean they don't exist. I can show you

God exists Tony, because I can show you how much he cares for you, how much he loves you.'

Tony felt deeply uncomfortable. This idea of 'love' bothered him. Until Aiya, he hadn't experienced it. His parents had never told him they loved him. They'd never shown him they loved him either. Jowmo had sometimes shown affection, but from the time he arrived in China Tony had had any notion of love beaten out of him by his grandfather. When Aiya came along she'd turned his world upside-down. She'd told him she loved him and for the first time ever he'd known it. It wasn't just a giddy rush of romance either. It was something much deeper. Aiya had made him feel wanted and special, like he'd never felt before. Yes, it was wonderful, but she'd gone. Love had been ripped out of him and he could barely stand the emptiness and the pain. He'd hardened himself again. Lowsi had been right. Tony didn't need anyone or anything, just his inner strength.

'Look Michael, I hear what you're saying, but even if your God does exist, there's no way he would want anything to do with me. You've no idea of the things I've done . . .'

'No, Tony, that's where you're wrong,' Michael interrupted. 'OK, you're behind bars, you got caught for your crimes and people out there think of you as a bad person, but listen to this, in God's eyes you and I are no different.'

'What? You're a goody two-shoes. God's best buddy.'

Michael grew serious. 'The Bible tells us that no one is perfect, Tony, that's why God sent his son, Jesus. God couldn't come near us because we are so imperfect. It's like when you spill just a tiny drop of black ink on a white shirt – the shirt is ruined. It doesn't matter whether it's a big black splodge of ink, or a tiny spot, that white shirt is spoiled either way.'

'So?'

'So – God created us, he longs to be our friend, Tony. He longs for us to love him the way he loves us and he wants us to live with him forever when we die. That's why he sent his son to become one of us.'

Tony shook his head. What was this gibberish?

'When Jesus came to earth as a man he was perfect,' said Michael, 'but he was put to death. He died a very cruel death on the cross, taking the punishment that you and I – every one of us – deserve. He was an innocent man, but he willingly took a life sentence for the people he loves so much. It was like somebody stepped into your place, Tony, leaving you to go free.'

Michael let his words hang in the air. He sensed that Tony was starting to listen.

'You can have that freedom now, Tony. And then, instead of rotting in the never-ending punishment you deserve, you also get a place in heaven when you die. That's if you choose to accept it. Do you ever think about that, Tony?'

'Hell can't be much worse than this,' Tony muttered, but he shuddered at the idea. He'd never thought about it much, but now he was beginning to wonder. What does happen when you die? Surely there was just nothing? Maybe it was like being asleep. Tony didn't like that idea. His sleep was always haunted by nightmares. Was this the hell people talked about? What if Michael was right? It made sense to him that there was more to life than this. Surely it couldn't all just end in blackness?

'It's as if we did the crime, but he served the time,' Michael smiled. 'Because of Jesus, God can forgive us for all the wrong things we have done – whether that's as big as armed robbery, or as small as stealing a pencil from school. Only God can set us free from the punishment we deserve, Tony. All you have to do is tell him how sorry you are and ask him to forgive you. Think again about that white shirt. Imagine Jesus makes you clean, no more black ink, just a perfect white shirt, perfect in God's eyes.

Tony wasn't sure. He still couldn't imagine anyone wanting to forgive him for the terrible crimes he'd committed, but Michael's talk of freedom was really getting to him.

'You talk of being set free, Michael, but look at me,' Tony spat. 'How can I be free?'

'You're not, Tony, but let me tell you, it's not the prison bars of Nicosia Central that are keeping you locked up. Even if you managed to break out tonight, you still wouldn't be free.'

'Of course I would. What are you talking about?'

'No, Tony, you would never be free from yourself, or from everything that drives you. You will never have the freedom that God can give you until you believe and accept what I'm telling you about his son, Jesus. The Bible tells us that if the Son sets you free, you will be free indeed. That's like nothing you've ever known.'

Tony clenched his fists in anger. He wanted to smash his way out of the rotten, stinking place there and then. Then he'd find out about freedom!

'Think about it like this, Tony. You've got a hole inside you that all your life you've been trying to fill up. You've driven yourself to be the best at everything. Maybe if you get out of here you'll work hard, get a great job, and even make some good friends. You'll earn loads of money, you'll get a fancy house and a car, the best computer, mobile phone . . . all these things, but I can promise you, none of it will make you truly happy. Even with all these things in your life, that hole will still be there.'

'I'd give it a go,' said Tony sarcastically, remembering the early days working as a bodyguard. He'd had all these things, but Michael was right, he'd still always wanted more. There was something inside that was never complete. He was always looking for the next thing, always trying to prove himself. And what had it all been for? Look how his life had ended up!

'Y'know, people say it's a God-shaped hole. Only God can fill it. Only he can make you truly happy. I promise you, Tony, if God sets you free it won't matter which side of the prison bars you are, you will have that freedom in your heart that no one can take away from you.'

Suddenly the bell rang. Visiting time was over.

Tony saw a look of dismay fly across Michael's face. He leaned forward so their faces were almost touching.

'You have a choice in all this, Tony. You can stay as you are, but if you put your trust in God, you will be amazed what he will do for you. He will never let you down. He is a father who loves you and will always be there for you. No matter how much I, or anyone else, care for you, there will be times when we will let you down, when we disappoint or hurt you. God will never do that. Please, Tony, make that choice. Make it now, today.'

Tony didn't know what to say. He could feel Michael's desperation. Suddenly he wanted to understand. He didn't want to be angry, but there was a huge battle going on inside his head.

'Tony, I know this is a lot to understand,' said Michael, 'but all you have to do is talk to God, either out loud, or in your heart. It's simple really. Just talk to him and be willing to turn away from the things that are wrong in your life. I know there are things you think you'll never be able to change, but God will help you if you are willing and if you ask him. Make God the most important person in your life, Tony, acknowledge that he's your boss, your master, and he will help you. He will show you how precious you are to him and how good your life can be.'

Tony looked down at the table.

'My friend, I could say so much more to you, but it's up to you and God.'

The room was beginning to empty.

'All you have to do is believe in him, Tony, please.'

Tony opened his mouth to say something, but no words would come.

Michael started to pray: 'Lord Jesus we thank you that you are here with us in this prison. Thank you that you love Tony so much. I pray that he will come to accept your love very soon. Amen.'

A guard came over, ushering Michael to leave. Tony couldn't look up. He felt so awkward.

'Tony, I will see you next week,' said Michael quietly, making his way out of the room.

Tony said nothing.

28

TAMING THE TIGER

Tony made his way quickly back along the prison wing. His mind was whirling with Michael's words. The stench from the block seemed worse than ever. One of the other men was crying, screaming and cackling to himself. The noise bounced off the walls, tormenting Tony's troubled mind all the more.

When he got to his cell, one of the lunatics was loitering outside. As Tony pushed past, the man dug his cigarette into Tony's arm, deeply scorching the flesh. Tony leaped back and then grabbed the man's hair, pushing his face into the wall. Fury rained down on him like hail and he beat the man beyond recognition.

Once in his cell, Tony began to tremble. He started to pace the floor, trying to stay in control. Michael's words were spinning round and round in his head. He screwed his eyes shut and covered his ears with his hands, trying to block the words out, but they would not go. His hands smelled of blood, and outside he could still hear the whimpering of the man he had just beaten. Suddenly he found himself thinking of Aiya and the way she'd been able to 'see' people with her hands. He remembered her tender touch on his face the first time they had met. He imagined her feeling the broken and bloodied face of the man outside. What would Aiya think of him now? She was the only person who had ever loved him, but he felt sure she would hate what he had become.

Tony flung himself on the bed, pulling the pillow around his ears to shut out the noise. Michael's words were still there: 'God loves you Tony; God loves you . . .' They ran over and over in his head. Although Tony wrestled to shut them out, as the minutes ticked by the words became strangely calming. Tony's breathing slowed and the words came more clearly than ever. Now there were more. 'God loves you so much that he sent his Son to die for you.' They seemed to be dropping into his head. 'You will be free . . . You will be free indeed . . . all you have to do is believe . . .'

'But how?' Tony cried out loud, as if shouting back at the words in his head. 'Where do I start?'

As if in answer, a picture of the man's broken face outside his cell appeared in his head. Suddenly Tony let out a pained and brutal cry. 'Sorry. Oh my God . . . I'm so sorry!'

With that, the floodgates came crashing down. Images of his life seemed to flash before him like a movie. Tony saw everyone he'd ever beaten or hurt. It was as though he was falling through a hideous, haunted tunnel of agony.

'I'm sorry,' he wailed, over and over again. Then the words changed. 'God, if you're there, please forgive me,' he wept.

The movie was running faster now. Tony fought to slow it down – to remember each and every crime so that he could cry out, saying he was sorry. Gasping for air, he knew that his cries were becoming louder and more frenzied. He pressed his face down into the pillow until it was sodden with his tears. On and on he cried, begging God to forgive him for *everything*.

Hours passed.

When Tony next raised his head the cell was in darkness. The door had been locked and the prison was quiet. Looking up through the tiny window Tony could see the moon in the night sky. His eyes focused on the iron bars and the cross shape they made where they joined. He remembered Michael telling him about Jesus' death on the cross. What was it he'd said? Something about because Jesus died, he could be set free. Tony still wasn't sure that he understood, but now, somehow, he knew it was true.

'I do believe in you,' Tony whispered quietly. 'I do believe you can save me. Thank you, Jesus.'

It was a simple prayer. And for the first time in his life Tony slept soundly and peacefully.

The next morning everything seemed different. For as long as he could remember, Tony had been angry – with his parents, with Lowsi, with the bullies at school, the list went on and on. Now that anger had gone. He felt calm. Sitting up in bed he looked again through the little window. It was a beautiful, sunny day. Tony realized that over the last few months he'd stopped even looking outside. He'd failed to notice the beautiful clear blue sky and the birds flying high above.

He felt strangely warm, even though the sun had yet to heat the stone walls of the prison block. He lay back for a while, thinking about the previous day, about Michael and the strange things that had happened in the evening.

Suddenly there was the sound of the door being unbolted. Leaping up from his bed he caught sight of a cigarette packet on the floor. Strangely, he'd not even thought about them yet this morning. He didn't need one at all. He smiled to himself and shook his head in disbelief, giving the packet a kick. No. He was fine. He definitely didn't want one.

A large, red-headed brute was standing just outside the door. Tony knew there could be trouble. They'd come to blows before. Tony's mind flashed back to the previous evening and he saw that there was still blood on the floor of the corridor. A bitter taste filled his mouth. Tony took a careful step forward and immediately the man swung round, laughing and stubbing a cigarette into Tony's arm.

Tony just looked him straight in the face, brushed the ash from his arm and walked away.

To his astonishment, when Tony got to the breakfast area, he realized there was nothing on his arm. No burn. No mark. No pain. He carefully examined where the burn should have been. There was nothing! What was going on?

Tony started thinking about some of the things Michael had told him during his visits. One day he'd arrived very excited, telling Tony he'd nearly been in a nasty car accident. Tony could still see him, all flustered and shaky. 'Tony, I thank God for his protection,' he had said. 'There is no way I could have avoided that truck. I really believe God looked after me so I could come here today.'

Then Tony found himself thinking about his school RE classes again. Mr Sizer had told them about Jesus healing people and feeding thousands from just a few pieces of bread and fish, even raising people from the dead. Tony had loved hearing these stories. 'Miracles,' Mr Sizer had called them. Was this the same Jesus? Was it because of Jesus that Tony's arm had been spared a nasty burn? Tony examined his arms and saw the scars from other such attacks. The one from the night before was still sore, but there was definitely nothing new.

Tony started smiling to himself, and then laughing. He couldn't help it. Now he was giggling like a child. Some of the other prisoners were looking at him, but they just assumed he was going mad, like many others before him.

What was this? Joy. Such deep, deep joy. It bubbled up from his stomach and made him tingle all over. Tony gripped the table for fear that he might soon get up and dance. He remembered Michael talking about the joy that was to be found in Jesus Christ. He'd talked about 'fullness of life'. Tony hadn't understood before, but now he was beginning to see. Believing in Jesus wasn't just an 'after life' issue. It wasn't just to do with what happens when you die. Now Tony realized what Michael had been trying to tell him all these months. With Jesus in his life, Tony was free, now, today! Even though he was in prison. Even though he had nothing. Even though his life was miserable, he now felt free and happier than ever before in his life!

A miracle? It had to be.

29

A MIRACLE

Tony's new-found joy barely faded in the days that followed, even though prison life was as hard as ever. It was infectious too.

One day Tony was sitting in the library. They called it a library, but there were few books there. They had disappeared years ago as fuel for the fires in the winter. It was a dark, dingy place, littered with dirty magazines. Hardly anyone went there, but now Tony enjoyed the quiet. He spent hours learning more about God and Jesus by reading his Bible. He wrote letters to Michael Wright on any bit of paper he could get his hands on. When they had first met, Michael had promised not to preach at Tony. Now Tony was hungry for Michael's wisdom. He had so many questions.

'What's up with you?' asked Shane.

Tony looked up, startled. He'd hardly noticed the thin Sri Lankan man coming into the library.

'What do you mean, mate?'

'Well, you're grinning all over your face.'

'Am I?' said Tony, still beaming.

'Yeah, I've been watching you for days. You got some new stuff or something?'

'What?' Tony knew what Shane meant. Shane was serving time for drug trafficking. There wasn't much he didn't know about illegal substances. He'd tried the lot and was a grade one addict.

Adrenaline pumped through Tony's veins. Could he tell Shane the truth? How could he not?

'Jesus,' he suddenly found himself saying.

'What? Not heard of that one,' said Shane. 'New word for crack is it?'

'No,' said Tony, laughing out loud. 'Listen, I know it will sound odd to you, but I've got Jesus in my life. I prayed to him the other night and I've never felt happier.'

Tony thought about what he'd just said. It was true, but he knew it sounded a little silly. He racked his brain to think of a way to explain things to Shane in a way he would understand. Shane was looking around, checking no one was watching, before taking out a small packet and a dirty-looking needle. That was Tony's lead.

'Look Shane, you don't need that stuff.' Shane looked up at him through hollow, red-rimmed eyes. Tony continued. 'Every time you take a hit, you feel good don't you?'

'Sure man,' replied Shane, carefully opening the packet and smelling the contents.

'But that good feeling wears off, doesn't it? You need more again, and then more. That's not happiness, Shane, it's addiction.'

'Do you think I don't know that?' said Shane lazily.

'But Jesus can set you free of that. He's done it with me.' Tony carried on talking, telling Shane what Michael had told him. To Tony's amazement, Shane was really interested. He didn't argue, the way Tony had with Michael. He just tried to understand.

'Hang on,' he interrupted at one point. 'I understand about God being holy and perfect and all that, but where does Jesus fit in?'

Tony thought for a while, and then started to tell Shane a story. 'Imagine there were two boys. They grew up together and were very close friends.'

'Yeah, OK.'

'Well, over the years they stuck together but, as they grew up, one of them fell into bad company. The other worked hard and got a good education. Eventually he became a top judge. Meanwhile, the other man started committing crimes and eventually he was caught. He ended up in court. The judge turned out to be his old friend, but at the time he didn't recognize him. The judge, however, instantly spotted that the criminal before him was his oldest and dearest friend who he loved very much.'

'What happened?' asked Shane, intrigued.

'Well, the man was clearly guilty and the judge had to punish him. That was what he deserved.'

'Yeah, understood.'

'Well, here's the thing,' smiled Tony. 'The judge knew that he had to either send him to prison or issue a large fine, which he knew his friend could not pay. So he passed sentence, then to the astonishment of the court he took off his judge's gown and his wig, and he went and stood in the dock with his friend. He then took out his cheque book and wrote a cheque to cover the fine.'

Tony waited, allowing Shane to work out the meaning of the story.

'So, the judge paid the debt for his old friend?' said Shane.

'Yes, but more than that,' said Tony. 'He was the judge, so he couldn't let the man off just because he knew him and loved him. Because of who he was, he was bound to see that a sentence was passed and that a punishment was issued. But because he loved the man so much, he decided to step down from being a judge. He became like the man in the dock and paid his debt for him.'

'And you're saying this is what God did for us?'

'Right. He had to become one of us to pay our debt. That's why God came down to earth, in his son, Jesus. Jesus then died, in our place, so that we could be saved from the punishment we deserved when we broke God's laws.'

'It was good of him, wasn't it?' said Shane quietly.

That made Tony laugh. 'Yes, it was good of him. So now, Shane, you have to decide if you believe all this. If you do, tell God. Tell him you believe Jesus died to take your place, so that you could be forgiven and set free.'

'I'll do it,' said Shane eagerly. 'What else?'

Tony hadn't expected such a quick reaction. 'Help me, God,' he prayed quickly, hoping he would say the right things to his friend.

'I guess I need to say sorry for everything, don't I?' said Shane.

'Yes, that's it,' said Tony, astonished. 'Then you need to ask God to help you turn away from the wrong things you do.' He thought back to one of Michael's letters. 'And you must be willing to surrender your life to God.'

'What does that mean?'

'Well, the Bible tells us that God knew each one of us, even before we were born. If you believe that and you believe he really is Almighty God, maker of everything, then surely he deserves to be the number one priority in your life.'

'Yeah, I get that, but what do you mean, "surrender"?'

Tony thought hard. 'All my life I've been the best at what I do. I was a kung fu world champion; I was a senior bodyguard; I would never admit I needed anybody else. It's like a boy who boasts that he can lift a big weight. He struggles and struggles until finally he has to surrender. He has to admit he needs help. He can't do it all alone. When he asks for help, that's surrendering himself.'

'I don't know if I'm strong enough to quit this stuff,' said Shane sadly, pushing the foil packet and the dirty needle tentatively aside. Tony didn't know what to say. He knew how tough drug addiction could be.

'That's something you and God will have to sort out together,' he said. 'But when you have him in your life, you will have a helper – you won't have to struggle in your own strength. If God wants you to quit, he will help you do it, if you ask him. All we can do is pray to God, asking him to help us, day to day.'

'Let's do it now,' said Shane.

Tony was nervous. He'd never prayed out loud before, the way Michael did. He barely knew what to say, but he drew closer to Shane, closed his eyes and started speaking. Soon Shane was joining in himself, in his own language. Tony opened his eyes and saw that Shane had tears streaming down his face. Still, his smile was one to rival Michael Wright's. Tony didn't have a clue what Shane was saying, but he knew it was a heartfelt prayer and he believed God would meet with Shane, just as he was doing with him.

Tony looked around the shabby dungeon. God had worked another miracle here. It was as though Jesus himself had been sitting next to him, helping him know what to say as he had talked to Shane. Now Tony was grinning all over his face. Was it really this wonderful? Was it really so easy to talk to God? Had he really answered Tony's prayer? Yes. No wonder Michael Wright said it was good news he wanted to give him.

At last Tony understood what had driven his friend to keep coming back week after week. I just wish I'd listened to Michael sooner, Tony thought. All these months I could have been living with this happiness, instead of desperate misery. It took me so long to trust him. All my life I was raised to trust no one. Look where it got me!

Tony shook his head, thinking how stubborn he'd been. He felt ashamed and stupid, but he knew now that God didn't think of him that way. He'd been given a new start and he had a feeling there were some exciting things in store for him.

30

FREE AT LAST!

In the weeks and months that followed, Tony shared his new joy with other prisoners. It was easy. Like Shane, many of them had noticed a sudden and startling difference in Tony. They all wanted to know what was going on with him, and day by day Tony grew more and more bold in telling them how he believed Jesus was changing his life. Even some of the toughest men ended up crying out to God. With Michael Wright's help, Tony set up a group where the men could study and learn from the Bible, and gather to pray whenever they could.

Tony looked around his cell one day. Men were squeezed into every available space. It was a comical sight. Big Ziggy, a drug smuggler, and Andreas, a Greek bodybuilder, were huddled together like sardines, trying to make space on the bed for Mohammed, Martin and Hassan. Others squatted on the floor. All were waiting for Tony to start their meeting with a prayer.

'Where's Shane?' asked Tony, noticing his friend was missing.

Just then the door burst open. It was Simone, another of the group. He was breathless and distressed.

'Alcaponey's had Shane,' he said, struggling to tell them what had happened.

Tony's blood ran cold. Pushing past Simone, he sped down the block towards Shane's cell. There were guards and a large group of prisoners standing outside, but it was eerily quiet. As he tried to push past the other men a group of four medics emerged from Shane's cell, carrying a stretcher.

'Shane?' shouted Tony, breaking the silence. 'Shane, mate!'

'Move aside,' ordered the guards. The other men parted, staring solemnly at the broken body on the stretcher. Tony thought he was going to be sick. He had never seen anyone so badly beaten.

A curtain of red-hot anger fell over him.

Tony hadn't felt his rage since that night he had first prayed to God in his cell. But now it was as though all that was forgotten. He was like a wild animal once again, fierce, furious and spitting. As the desperate sight of his friend disappeared he vowed revenge, promising to break Alcaponey into a million pieces.

✢ ✢ ✢

Tony couldn't talk to anyone for days afterwards and he hid from the others. He wanted to think about one thing. He wanted revenge. He wanted Alcaponey's blood.

Alcaponey was one of the lunatics. Shane wasn't his first victim, but Tony swore that he would be the last. Word got round about Tony's rage and Alcaponey knew he was after him. Both men were just waiting for their moment.

Nicosia Central Prison had many dead-end corridors and blocked-up ancient passageways. They were forbidding, dangerous places, but in the new darkness of his mind, Tony started seeking them out. Lurking in the silent squalor he wrestled with his rage and plotted his revenge. There was no room for God here. Once again, Tony was alone with his demons of destruction.

Suddenly a bloodcurdling yell bounced off the walls. Alcaponey's heaving form came out of the darkness. He was a huge brute, built like a house, serving a life sentence for multiple murders.

So he's been stalking me, Tony realized, blood beginning to surge in his veins. Good. Now's the time!

The passage was narrow and there was nowhere to go. Tony had no time to plan his defence. Before he could even think, Alcaponey was upon him, pinning him up against the wall. Tony could smell his stinking breath as he was lifted off the floor, level with Alcaponey's face. The men locked each other in a stare.

Tony called on his kung fu training, anticipating Alcaponey's next move. Though he was pinned by his arms, Tony knew he could quickly reach round and with one swift action rip at the brute's ear . . . But suddenly words seemed to appear in Tony's head:

Then the men stepped forward, seized Jesus and arrested him. With that, one of Jesus' companions reached for his sword, drew it out and struck the servant of the high priest, cutting off his ear.

What was this? The words continued:

'Put your sword back in its place,' Jesus said to him, 'for all who draw the sword will die by the sword. Do you think I cannot call on my Father, and he will at once put at my disposal more than twelve legions of angels?'

Tony realized this was a story he had read in his Bible. It was the account of Jesus' arrest before he was put to death on a cross. Now, in the heat of Alcaponey's attack, the words from the Bible had flooded into his mind.

Only a split second passed. Alcaponey was laughing, cackling like the madman he was, inviting Tony to make his move before he crushed him.

'Come on. Fight! You can take him,' yelled a voice in Tony's head.

Yet there was another voice.

'I am the way and the truth and the life.'

Tony recognized this. They were Jesus' words. Alcaponey's face was even closer now and Tony could taste the salt of his sweat. Something seemed to be holding Tony back, stopping him from making a move. He could call on the way of kung fu and beat the beast into a pulp. Surely that was the right thing to do?

'Yes, yes, do it for Shane. Do it for your friend,' rang the first voice in his head.

'I am the way. *I* am the way . . .' came a quiet whisper, '. . . the truth, the life.'

Suddenly words formed in Tony's mouth. He heard himself speak loud and clear into the darkness. Immediately his lust for Alcaponey's blood disappeared.

'In the name of Jesus Christ, I command you to leave me alone.' It was Tony's voice, but he barely recognized it. Alcaponey's face suddenly froze in terror and he dropped Tony to the floor.

Moments later Tony was alone and shaking. Leaning against the wall, he slowly slid down until he rested on the cold, damp floor, elbows on his knees and head in his hands.

What had happened? Minutes went by. Alcaponey was nowhere to be seen. Bewildered and dazed, Tony ran over the attack in his head, trying to make sense of it all.

'God has saved me,' he whispered to himself, in utter amazement.

It was true.

Tony hardly knew how to explain what had happened, but everyone was desperate to know what had gone on. They'd expected a blood bath; instead Alcaponey had fled and Tony had emerged out of the darkness completely unharmed. More than that, his rage seemed to have disappeared. It was clear something amazing had happened. When Tony told them the truth about how Jesus had saved him, some were bewildered, but many of the others had put their trust in God too. They knew it was true.

As for Tony, he came to realize something more . . . finally the Tiger had been set free.

POSTSCRIPT

Cry of the Tiger is a true story. Tony Anthony was sent to live in China when he was only four years old. Raised on his grandfather's cane, he became highly skilled in martial arts and achieved things that many would consider supernatural. The small, helpless boy became a tough man of great strength and physical power. Yet, as his story shows, this was to become his greatest weakness.

On 3 May 1990, while incarcerated in Nicosia Central Prison, Tony Anthony became a child again . . . a child of God. All his life Tony had craved the love, approval and acceptance of his family, only to be let down. Now he had a new and perfect Father, who loved him despite everything he had done.

Tony's encounter with Alcaponey taught him that a life surrendered to God is a life protected by him. Tony did not use kung fu, nor did he require the power of the chi to make him strong. It was God who worked a miracle, saving him from Alcaponey without a drop of blood being shed. Tony also learned that he was still free to go his own way. He was a *child* of God, not a *slave*. He was still able to make his own choices and capable of making big mistakes. After Shane's beating he had turned back to his rage and anger, hiding his face from his heavenly Father, but God did not turn away from him. Instead, he walked with Tony in the dark places, stood by him in his grief and saved him from himself. Nicosia was not the end of Tony's time in prison . . . but that's another story.

☩   ☩   ☩

Today Tony travels the world telling his story. Older readers can find out more about him in the international bestseller, *Taming the Tiger*, published by Authentic Media in 2004.

For more information about Tony Anthony's work see
www.avantiministries.com or you can contact him at
tony@avantiministries.com.